Walking
in the
Truth

Walking in the Truth

Perseverers and Deserters

THE FIRST, SECOND, AND
THIRD LETTERS OF JOHN

Gerard S. Sloyan

THE NEW TESTAMENT IN CONTEXT
Howard Clark Kee and J. Andrew Overman, editors

TRINITY PRESS INTERNATIONAL
Valley Forge, Pennsylvania

Trinity Press International, P.O. Box 851, Valley Forge, PA 19482-0851

Library of Congress Cataloging-in-Publication Data

Sloyan, Gerard Stephen, 1919–
    Walking in the truth : perseverers and deserters : the First, Second, and Third letters of John / Gerard S. Sloyan.
      p. cm. — (New Testament in context)
    ISBN 1-56338-128-1 (alk. paper)
    1. Bible. N.T. Epistles of John—Commentaries. I. Title.
II. Series.
    BS2805.3.S63 1995
    227'.94077–dc20   95-24861
                                 CIP

Printed in the United States of America

95 96 97 98 99   10 9 8 7 6 5 4 3 2 1

I was overjoyed to find some of your children
walking in the truth. . . .

—2 John 4

Contents

Introduction to the Letters

The most certain thing that can be said about the three epistles of John is that they were composed by a person or persons in the circle, perhaps the "school," out of which came the Gospel according to John. Of them all, only 3 John is unequivocally in letter form, much like St. Paul's brief communication to Philemon. There the subject was a plea to that wealthy believer to take back his runaway slave, whom Paul in prison had "begotten" in faith. Gaius in 3 John hears from someone he knows so well that "the elder" will do as an identification. After the elder commends Gaius for his hospitality toward itinerant believers ("the brothers" or "friends"), he complains to him about a certain Diotrephes, who has been rebuffing both them and him.

Bultmann in his 1967 commentary on the epistles (2d ed.) thinks that the letter form of 2 John should probably be taken as a fiction. He finds its content demonstrably derivative from the Gospel of John but thinks the letters from "the elder" to another church designated the "elect lady" is a device calculated to record, once a plea for communal love has been entered, a bitter complaint against "antichrist." These are the "deceivers" who have gone beyond the main body of believers, who in turn remain in the teaching of Christ. That teaching, in context, does not seem to be Jesus' remembered words but the tradition about him that holds that he has come in the flesh.

1 John seems the least letter-like of the three in its lack of the identification of a sender or an address to any recipients except the non-specific "little children." It appears to be more a treatise sent broadcast to some in the John tradition who are either tempted to depart from certain heretofore solid doctrinal under-

standings or are threatened by those who have seceded from the community. The content of the tradition is both taken for granted and spelled out afresh. The "antichrist" is a liar, denying that Jesus has come in the flesh. With the blood of God's Son Jesus, said to cleanse us from all sin, we have a theology of redemption not found in the Fourth Gospel.

Each of the three short pieces is a different sort of writing. That by no means indicates that three different authors are at work, for different purposes can call for different writing styles. It is common to attribute all three epistles to the same author, a person other than the final editor of the Gospel. No reason exists, however, to demand single authorship. The case for a common author of 2 and 3 John but not the First Epistle is somewhat stronger, although even there the writer of the second may be emulating the style of the third. Whoever the writer or writers were, they have in common a familiarity with the ideas expressed in John's Gospel, but they do not necessarily know its text. Indeed 1 John, which is the longest, will use words and phrases from that writing in different senses than the evangelist's.

Beginning early in this century von Dobschütz, then Bultmann and Braun, have supposed that this epistle was cobbled together from different sources. The theory is based on the assumption of a perfect consistency in style that 1 John, brief as it is, does not exhibit. Bultmann thinks it could have ended at 2:27, indeed did so at one point, after which a number of admonitions have been added about sin and lawlessness, mutual love and the love that comes from God expressed in the sending of the Son as an atoning sacrifice for our sins. While it is impossible to say that sources were not drawn on, the differing styles of the earlier and later parts of the letter do not tell definitively against its composition by one person.

The most surprising feature of these writings to one who has not previously been familiar with them is their harshness of tone. Most Christians have a hearsay acquaintance with John as a Gospel of love. They are also likely to have heard something like this from 1 John in whatever context: "The person who does not love does not know God, for God is love. God's love was revealed among us in this way: God sent his only Son into the world so that we might live through him" (1 John 4:8-9); "We love because God first loved us" (4:19). There is much like this in the epistle but also vituperative passages like those against false prophets who are antichrists (4:1, 3), sinners who are children of the devil (3:8), and murderers who do not love a brother or a sister (3:10, 15). The obloquy directed against religious deviants in the ancient world is a familiar story. Those who are deemed wrong in religion are accused of the grossest moral lapses, often making it impossible to determine what their sin or sins might have been. The "liar" of 1 John is one who denies that Jesus is the Christ. Such a one is the clear target of this epistle. He denies the Father as well as the Son (2:22).

We may ask what is being said here. What is the lie and what form exactly does the denial take? It seems clear that Jesus' having come in the flesh is the great matter at issue (4:2), his capability of having been seen and heard and touched if only through the report of revelation received (1:1-3). Does the hatred of fellow believers alluded to consist in calling this in question? A simple docetic outlook, namely, that he seemed to be human but was not, has been the judgment of Christian history on the sin of the seceders. But it could have been more subtle and more specific than that. The opponents may have believed that Jesus was a man in the flesh but not that he had come in order to die in the flesh, that is, to make atoning sacrifice by his blood (1:7; 4:6-8). They may have thought that faith in the Spirit and the water of baptism brought redemption (see 4:6-12). This may be their darkness and the full Johannine faith in redemption by blood the light in which they did not walk (1:6-7).

The most usual interpretation put on the three epistles is that they were written in the sequence 1, 2, and 3 and came after the Gospel. The first one is taken to have been an attempt to remove certain confusions the Gospel created, possibly the belief that it taught a Christ of Spirit who proposed baptism but whose death was a needless addition to faith in him as the redeeming Christ and Son of God. In such an understanding, 1 John was written in clearer terms than the Gospel of John to stem an exodus from the community that was already a threatening reality: those who have "gone out from us" (2:19). Letters 2 and 3 then come from the same writer at a later date or dates, probably as the "progressives" (2 John 9) move toward a gnostic position. They deliver the same doctrinal warning as 1 John but give specific counsel about receiving believers as guests and refusing hospitality to those who do not profess traditional Johannine faith.

The present writer has great respect for proponents of this theory but does not espouse it or indeed any other on the circumstances of composition. The attempt here is simply to explore what the three epistles may be saying when their meaning is obscure and to make accessible their message to the church of the present when it is not. There are so many echoes of biblical passages from both Testaments in this brief body of literature that it would be tedious to cite them all. A selection has been made. The remarkable thing is how much of it from the Newer Testament is extra-Johannine.

Rudolf Bultmann's commentary on the Johannine epistles, now almost thirty years old, is of great help in matters of grammar and syntax. It is, at many points, a dialogue with Rudolf Schnackenburg's earlier work, pointing out certain changes of opinion between that commentary's first and second editions. Bultmann makes liberal use of a bibliographical round-up done in 1940 by Ernst Haenchen in two issues of the journal *Theologische Rundschau*. The familiar Bultmann convictions are in evidence: that the Gospel of John is directed against "the world" represented by Pilate and those Jews who do not believe in Jesus; that 1 John is carrying on a polemic against unidentified gnostics; and that 2 John is evidence of an evolving "early Catholicism" (*Frühkatholizismus*), not a good development in Bultmann's eyes. The decisive argument against the common authorship of the Gospel and the First Epistle is taken to be their polemic on different fronts: against false teachers within the community in the case of the epistle and against outsiders in the case of the Gospel. Bultmann thinks that a prior written Source, which the author annotated, underlies 1 John. The author edited it ecclesiastically (not meant as a term of praise). Of the whole epistle, 1:1–2:27 was originally an independent writing, "or perhaps more appropriately a rough draft, to which individual sections dealing with the same themes as in the earlier part were added" (Introduction, p. 2).

The English translation of Schnackenburg's commentary is based on the seventh German edition (1984; 2d ed., 1960). The author notes the ample literature on the Johannine epistles and Gospel that appeared since the sixth edition of five years before, including a supplementary fourth volume to his *The Gospel According to St. John* (ET, 1968–82), which has not yet been translated. He also identifies Raymond E. Brown's *The Epistles of St. John* (1982) as "the most important event that has occurred" since he produced the latest edition of his *Johannine Epistles* (Preface, p. xi). Although the latter runs to only three hundred pages in translation, its attention to the textual witness, stylistic devices, and format of the epistles is rivaled only by the footnoted dialogue with the authors of a vast amount of literature. Schnackenburg thinks that the arguments for the unity of 1 John (including the author's editings) are stronger than those of a Source followed by the editings of the author and a subsequent editor. He finds the gnostic movement in the ascendant at the time of the writing and the author of 1 John secure in his christological and soteriological confessions in rebuttal, difficult as it is to determine the kind of gnosis his opponents adhered to. A major strength of this commentary is its multiple citations of the two Testaments. Following up on them is an excellent way to discover how the gospel was being presented late in the first century and how it was received or rejected within and outside the communities of Johannine influence.

Brown's Anchor Bible Commentary runs to more than eight hundred pages. As in his two-volume work on John's Gospel and his study of the first two chapters of Matthew and Luke and the Lukan genealogy (3:23–38) in *The Birth of the Messiah*, he provides his own translation of the three epistles, passage by passage. He then follows each of these with Notes, Comment, and Pertinent Bibliography to the passage. Brown's expansive style is marked by utter clarity and a gift for exposing all opinions, ancient and modern, on a knotty phrase before expressing his own. This commentary has no equal in wrestling with obscure locutions that other authors tend to by-pass. Brown is convinced that the epistles represent a life-and-death struggle between two groups of Johannine disciples over "their ideas about Jesus, about the Christian life, about eschatology, and about the Spirit" (Preface, p. xi). "The profound and innovative christology of GJohn," he maintains, contained dangers that led to a more "progressive" (2 John 9) evaluation of Jesus than the tradition represented by the epistles could allow (see ibid.). No commentator goes so far as Brown in speculating about the follow-up to the thought of the Gospel in the various John communities.

The compact commentary of J. L. Houlden (1973) is representative of others of this genre in the bibliography below: judicious, dependable, and (in this case) relying largely on British scholarship. Different from the rest is Charles Talbert's fifty-five-page treatment of the epistles in the order 2, 3, then 1 John. He presents this before attending to the Gospel on the hypothesis that various controversies recorded in the epistles imply that the Gospel was written alongside or after them. Grayston likewise thinks that 1 John was written before the Fourth Gospel. Quite different from the mainstream is *The Theology of the Johannine Epistles,* Judith Lieu's properly titled slim book on the theology of the epistles rather than a verse commentary. Her second chapter is given the same heading as the book title and takes up more than half of the text. Subheadings in that chapter include: "We know: confidence in the life of the community"; " 'Fellowship with him': the language of religious experience"; "Jesus in tradition and faith"; and "God and the world: election and dualism." Like other authors, Lieu employs the title of R. Law's 1909 commentary on 1 John, *The Tests of Life,* to describe the way Christian conduct is treated in the letters. She concludes with a few pertinent pages on their contemporary significance. For a bibliography of these and other works, see pp. 77–78 below.

In all, the field is so richly planted that it is an exercise in arrogance to attempt to harvest an additional yield. The present writer's comfort must be the ancient tag line, *Non nova sed nove.* There is nothing new in what follows but one thing or another may be expressed, without novelty, in a new way.

A word of appreciation to the Franciscan Friars of the Atonement, Washington, D.C, is in order here, for it was while living among them as a professorial lecturer at the Catholic University of America that these lines were written.

Chapter One _____

The First Letter of John

As is the case with a number of New Testament writings, we do not know who the author of the document called the First Letter of John is (hereafter 1 John) or to whom it was addressed. All we can be sure of is that it came out of the Johannine circle and was a warning to those within that circle about others who had departed from it. It stressed the truth of the tradition as the writer saw it. The separatists are referred to in extremely bitter terms. This comes as a surprise in a communication that is so insistent on God's love and the love that community members should have for one another. At the same time, the precise expression which that reciprocal love should take is the very point at issue. Hence, it should not come as a complete surprise that the case is argued with vigor, not to say asperity.

Those whom the writer castigates are wrong on two counts, he is convinced, one doctrinal and the other ethical. They do not believe in Jesus Christ as they ought, and they fail to keep his commandments. The writer of 1 John is quite sure that he knows what right faith and right conduct are. Unfortunately, he does not get specific about exactly what it is that separates him from those he so strongly opposes. It is obvious that both parties hold much of Johannine faith in common, meaning what is enunciated in the Fourth Gospel. That fact serves to obscure the precise differences between the Gospel and the epistles.

Students of 1 John are fairly widely agreed that this letter, as we shall call it, even though it does not have the usual form of a letter (greeting, identification of sender and recipient, message, and conclusion) opens with a preface or prooemium composed of the first four verses. They read as follows:

1   ¹We declare to you what was from the beginning, what we have heard, what we have seen with our eyes, what we have looked at and touched with our hands, concerning the word of life — ²this life was revealed, and we have seen it and testify to it, and declare to you the eternal life that was with the Father and was revealed to us — ³we declare to you what we have seen and heard so that you also may have fellowship with us; and truly our fellowship is with the Father and with his Son Jesus Christ. ⁴We are writing these things so that our joy [some early NT manuscripts read "your"; the difference in Greek, as in English, is one letter] may be complete.

Clearly the writer is at home in Johannine thought. It is not so clear that he knows the text of the Gospel of John (hereafter GJohn). If he knows it, he is not constrained in these early remarks to retain in their Gospel form any of its characteristic phrases besides "eternal life." Other echoes and words proper to the prologue of GJohn occur: "the beginning," "word," and "life" — but none of them appears in the same context as in the Gospel. Moreover, "word" here is not the *lógos* of the preface to GJohn but the message about the "life" brought by the enfleshed Word. The writer announces his purpose, namely, that those who hear his declaration may have fellowship or a life in common with the ones in whose name he speaks. This fellowship is a life similar to that already enjoyed by the writer "with the Father and with his Son Jesus Christ" (the latter combination is distinctly not a GJohn phrase). There will be no hint later that the recipients of this communication are being invited to anything new to them. They are presumed to possess this common life already and are being exhorted to continue and grow in it.

Is "what was from the beginning" the same "beginning" as in GJohn (1:1)? Seemingly not. The latter beginning, which syntactically is as indefinite as the one in the opening line of Genesis, seems to be in the innermost reaches of godhead, going back to the Son's lying "close to the Father's heart" (John 1:18). The beginning 1 John speaks of is apparently the inauguration of the mystery that he and his hearers or readers are privy to: "Jesus Christ come in the flesh" (4:2). This Jesus is someone the writer has seen and heard and touched. Immediately the question arises, does he make a claim to have known Jesus in his pre- and post-resurrected states? At first it seems so, so graphic is the wording. Closer inspection discloses the writer's purpose, which is to affirm the reality of the divine in palpable, physical form and to do so by giving public witness to this reality. Here the "we" is not the editorial we. It is used to identify the group that has received eyewitness testimony to the incarnation and been commissioned to pass it on. The "life" these verses testify to is, in the first place, Jesus himself (see John 11:25), who was made known by a "revelation" (1:2; cf. John 1:31). The life is none other than "the eternal life that was with the Father" (v. 2). Here the Johannine coexistence of Father and Son, Jesus Christ the life (v. 3), is unequivocally attested to. Such is the common life the two possess that was "revealed to us." It is not said, so much as implied, that the revealed life has created the fellowship that the writer enjoys with the Father and the Son. The life he has in common with God and other believers understandably causes him joy. The more intensely the life is lived, the greater will be the joy experienced.

These opening verses may be, as Raymond E. Brown suggests (*The Epistles of John,* p. 148), a reinterpretation of the GJohn prologue written to refute adversaries who are distorting its meaning.

THE GOSPEL ALREADY PROCLAIMED

1 ⁵This is the message [gospel] we have heard from him and proclaim to you, that God is light and in [God] there is no darkness at all.

The revealer from whom the gospel was first heard can only be the one who was experienced by hearing and sight and touch. This Jesus delivered the message (*aggelía;* 1:5 and 3:11 are its only New Testament usages) that is here being "proclaimed" (in a verb cognate with *aggelía*). In GJohn Jesus is called not only the light but the true light (1:4, 5, 9). Nineteen of the twenty-three times the Gospel uses the word "light" it applies to Jesus. The idea is expanded in the story of the raising of Lazarus: "The light is with you for a little longer. Walk while you have the light, so that the darkness may not overtake you.... While you have the light believe in the light, so that you may become children of light" (12:35a,b, 36). Nowhere in the Gospel, however, is God referred to as light except insofar as the divine light is manifested in Jesus. The letter recasts the GJohn material in the form "God is light," calling it "the gospel." God is here defined by activity or function. As revealer God illumines, gives light.

The First Testament associates the figure of light with God in several places, among them Psalm 4:6[7], Habakkuk 3:4, Isaiah 10:17, 60:19–20, and Wisdom 7:26. The sharp opposition between light and darkness appears initially in pseudepigraphic writings, e.g., the Testament of Naphthali, 2:10: "You are unable to perform the works of life while you are in darkness"; Test. Levi, 19:1: "And now, my children.... choose for yourselves light or darkness, the Law of the LORD or the works of Beliar." The Dead Sea Scrolls make the dualistic opposition much more graphic, featuring angelic princes of light and darkness who govern human beings (1QS 3:20–21). There is also the tract *The War of the Sons of Light and the Sons of Darkness* (1QM). The strong declaration of 1 John 1:5 that, in the gospel it proclaims, there is no darkness in God suggests that there are other gospels abroad — specifically, one other — that teach some measure of *skotía,* darkness in God. There will be more on this light-darkness opposition in 2:8–11. Meantime, it should be remembered that this is the way the author conceives the gospel he is proclaiming: it is the light of God versus the darkness of other messages that are abroad.

A WARNING AGAINST SIN,
THE BARRIER TO FELLOWSHIP WITH GOD

1 **6**If we say that we have fellowship with [God] while we are walking in darkness, we lie and do not do what is true; **7**but if we walk in the light as he himself is in the light, we have fellow-

ship with one another, and the blood of Jesus Christ cleanses us from all sin. [8]If we say that we have no sin, we deceive ourselves, and the truth is not in us. [9]If we confess our sins, he who is faithful and just will forgive us our sins and cleanse us from all unrighteousness. [10]If we say that we have not sinned, we make him a liar, and his word is not in us. 2 [1]My little children, I am writing these things to you so that you may not sin. But if anyone does sin, we have an advocate with the Father, Jesus Christ the righteous; [2]and he is the atoning sacrifice for our sins, and not for ours only but also for the sins of the whole world.

The pastoral concerns of the letter come through very clearly in this section. The writer knows that sin is a possibility even among those who enjoy fellowship with the Father and the Son. He will not let them live in a dream world, entertaining a euphoria that tells them they are beyond the failings of ordinary mortals. They are nothing of the sort. *Corruptio optimi pessima* is a proverb the writer is not likely to have heard, but he certainly knows its meaning: "The downfall of the best is the worst." Those who have once heeded the high calling of membership in the believing community can tragically fall away from it. They must be warned. Better still, they must be told the remedy that lies ready to hand.

To claim fellowship with God while walking in darkness is to lie, to deviate from the truth. This, evidently, is the path others have chosen. What is their sin, their elected "darkness"? We are not yet told. We must read on. If we look ahead to 2:19 we discover that there are certain people well known to the writer who "went out from us.... By going out they made it plain that none of them belongs to us." As that passage continues, the hearer learns why the speaker thinks them liars, people who no longer do the truth. But at this early stage of the epistle, 1:6–2:2, we are not told.

The phrase "doing the truth" (v. 6) is a Semitic expression found twice in the Hebrew Bible, in Nehemiah 9:33 and 2 Chronicles 31:20, where it refers to God's keeping faith and to Hezekiah's fidelity to the law. GJohn employs the phrase, fairly common in postbiblical literature and the Qumrân scrolls, in 3:21a: "The one who does the truth comes into the light." Noteworthy is the introductory verb in vv. 6, 8, and 10, which is perhaps better rendered "If we boast" or "claim" than "say." The declaration of sinlessness or possessing fellowship with God while one walks in darkness is false. Walking in the light as God is in light is the condition of fellowship with one another (see 1:3b). This walking in light has been made possible by being cleansed from sin by God's Son, Jesus (v. 7c).

His death as a sacrifice for human sinfulness is a muted theme in GJohn, his blood as shed occurring only in 10:34. This epistle and Revelation make much more of the blood of Christ, respectively in 5:6, 8 and 1:5, 5:9, 7:14, and 12:11. As to the capacity of Christ's blood to cleanse from sin, 1 John probably has in mind the annual smearing of the altar with the blood of a sacrificed beast. "For on this day atonement shall be made for you, to cleanse you; from all your sins you shall be clean before the LORD" (Lev. 16:30); "I have given [blood] to you for making atonement for your lives on the altar; for, as life, it is the blood that makes atonement" (17:11b,c). GJohn does, of course, speak of Jesus as the lamb who takes away the sin of the world (1:29) and of cleansing by washing or bathing (13:10–11) but not by blood. Here, cleansing of all sin by Christ's blood is assumed to be a well-known teaching in the Johannine churches.

The self-deception indulged in by those who say they have no sin (v. 8) has been mentioned above. To "have sin" (v. 8) means to be guilty of sin and is the diametric opposite of "having fellowship" (v. 3), which "walking in the light" (v. 7) brings about. The "truth" that is in us is an interiorized principle of Godlike fidelity that comes with following Christ who is the truth. To claim oneself free of sin is to depart from that truth. In the mind of the writer all have sinned and need to acknowledge their sins. If they do so, the God who is faithful and just (v. 9; cf. Deut. 7:9; John 17:25 for these adjectives) will forgive them and cleanse them from all wrongdoing. The latter word, *adikía*, was chosen by the author in direct contrast to God as the just one, *díkaios*. The claimant of sinlessness makes a liar of God (v. 10; cf. 5:10), who has sent Jesus to take away a world's sin.

Obviously, dissuasion from sin is as much the intent of 1 John as reminding those who receive the letter that, although cleansed from the guilt of sin, they must nonetheless confess it. The writer says as much, addressing them affectionately as "little children" (2:1; cf. 2:12, 28; 3:7, 18; 4:4; 5:21; the same diminutive form of the word for child will describe "children of God" in 3:1, 2, 10, and 5:2). In the tragic event of sin by members of the community, the writer goes on to say, they need not despair. They have an advocate. The word is *paráklētos,* as in John 14:16, 26; 15:26; 16:7. Even though the Spirit is called "another Paraclete" at the first appearance of the term in GJohn, making Jesus an earthly advocate "with the Father," here in 1 John 1:2 Jesus speaks to God on behalf of sinners from his place in heaven. Moreover, when the Spirit of God (4:2) or the Spirit of truth (v. 6) is later referred to there is no acknowledgment that the term *paráklētos* is associated with this Spirit. It is a Jesus Christ term in 1 John.

As "atoning sacrifice" (*hilasmós,* 2:2; cf. 4:10) he is priest and victim in a heavenly temple rather than a pleader in the heavenly court. This figure echoes the earlier one of his cleansing us by his blood (1:7). The word "atonement" means bringing into one two who have been at odds. While the temple's sacrifices achieved this for sinners or a sinful Israel in relation to God, *hilasmós* might better be translated here as "expiation." That word connotes cleansing or doing away with guilt. It includes, in certain First Testament uses, the notion of placating a wrathful God but does not do so here. The name of the annual feast of Leviticus 25:9, *Yom kippurîm* in Hebrew, is *hilasmós* in the Septuagint. The cognate *hilastérion* of Romans 3:25 and Hebrews 9:5 is the mercy seat or propitiatory of the LXX, the surface of beaten gold placed above the ark with cherubim at either side. But Jesus is not here spoken of under that figure. He is *hilasmós,* literally victim but also by implication a priest, whose sacrifice achieves the salvation of the world (2:2; cf. John 4:42).

Knowing God and Obeying God's Commandments

2 ³Now by this we may be sure that we know [God], if we obey God's commandments. ⁴Whoever says, "I have come to know [God]," but does not obey the commandments of God, is a liar, and in such a person the truth does not exist; ⁵but whoever obeys [God's] word, truly in this person the love of God has reached perfection. By this we may be sure that we are in [God]: ⁶whoever says, "I abide in [God]," ought to walk just as [Jesus Christ] walked.

⁷Beloved, I am writing you no new commandment, but an old commandment that you have had from the beginning: the old commandment is the word that you have heard. ⁸Yet I am writing you a new commandment that is true in Christ and in you, because the darkness is passing away and the true light is already shining. ⁹Whoever says, "I am in the light," while hating a brother [or sister] is still in the darkness. ¹⁰Whoever loves a brother [or sister] lives in the light, and in such a person there is no cause for stumbling. ¹¹But whoever hates another believer is in the darkness, walks in the darkness, and does not know the way to go, because the darkness has brought on blindness.

A practical test is proposed for any who say they "know God." Surely some adversarial faction has made this boast, some believers in Christ who think that people like the writer are just so many earth-bound plodders. Theirs is a superior knowledge. They may even be called "proto-gnostics," forerunners of what has been called the most serious challenge to the faith of the apostolic age. It will blossom toward the third quarter of the second century. At this date, however, there already seem to be claimants to know God, even to see God (see 3:6), whom the writer knows to be abysmal failures when it comes to the test of conduct. Up to this point 1 John has had a negative character in its warnings against falling into sin or "walking in darkness." Indeed, 2:4 is an echo of 1:6 and 8 with its antithesis of lies and truth. The present section, however, proposes the right way to go. It names keeping God's commandments as the sure proof of the love of God, which in some has come to perfection (v. 5a, an objective genitive meaning love *for* God). This observance is at the same time the means to be sure of God's love for us that has been revealed in Christ. Those who obey God's commandments are the only ones qualified to say they know God. Those who fail the test of obedience are simply liars. The writer does not claim fidelity to these precepts for the members of his fellowship. He always expresses it conditionally lest they depart from the truth in their boasting. But he is quite sure who is making the lying claim. He knows them by the fruits they have not produced. He proposes a test that his fellow devotees should apply to themselves. Do they say: "I abide in Him"? Here the context requires that Christ, not God, be the referent. Those who presume to say it must let their pattern of life be as his was.

There are no solid grounds for thinking that the early part of 1 John just commented upon existed initially as a baptismal homily. At the same time, its phrasing has much in common with the terms of entry into the covenant community of Qumrân and with Christian initiatory practice found elsewhere in the Second Testament. Thus, in Acts 26:18 Jesus says to Paul in the third account this book provides of Paul's conversion to Christ, spoken before King Agrippa: "I am sending you [to the Gentiles] to open their eyes so that they may turn from darkness to light and from the power of Satan to God." Colossians 1:13–14 has a similar view of conversion to belief in Christ: "[God] has rescued us from the power of darkness and transferred us into the kingdom of his beloved Son, in whom we have redemption, the forgiveness of sins." Ephesians 5:7–8 comes very close to the warnings contained in 1 John: "Therefore do not be associated with [the disobedient, deceivers with empty words]. For once you were darkness, but now in the Lord you are light. Live as children of light."

Unfortunately we do not possess the earliest mode in which formation in Christ leading to baptism was preached nor any of the rites of initiation employed in the first sixty or seventy years. These exhortations give us a clue, however, to what may have gone on in the decades before writings like Acts 2–4. 1 John is of this genre: a reminder of the clean break with the life that preceded baptism and a stern admonition not to slip back into it—or to deceive oneself into thinking that one has gone beyond it. Perfectionism has always had an attraction for the pious, for intellectuals, for those who are confident they have mastered the basics. 1 John teaches that perfection consists in obeying God's word, that and nothing else (2:5).

In this context the "word" or *lógos* of God is all that has been revealed in Christ. It includes his commandments, which were, of course, an insight into and a reframing of the Mosaic commands. The term "word" occurs in both the singular and the plural in GJohn. There, Jesus keeps the Father's word; the disciples keep Jesus' word and also the Father's word. In one characteristic passage Jesus says: "They who have my commandments and keep them are those who love me.... Those who love me will keep my word, and my Father will love them.... Whoever does not love me does not keep my words; and the word that you hear is not mine, but is from the Father who sent me" (John 14:21a, 23b,c, 24).

The claim "I abide in him" of 1 John 2:6 employs a favorite verb of GJohn (forty times). In the Gospel it is used to describe the continued dwelling of the believer in God, in Jesus, and in Jesus and the Father; likewise, the dwelling of God and of Jesus in the believer and of the Father in Jesus. Conducting oneself as Jesus did is 1 John's test for this abiding or dwelling in God.

There are a couple of other places in the Christian Scriptures where Jesus is proposed as the model for his followers, but they do not use the adverb "just as" of v. 6b. St. Paul in Romans 15:5 exhorts the members of that community to "live in harmony with one another, in accordance with [*katà*] Jesus Christ," while Hebrews 12:2 encourages believers to run the race with perseverance, "looking to Jesus the pioneer and perfecter of our faith, who...endured the cross, disregarding its shame." The invitation in 1 John to walk as Jesus did is a clear call to imitate his conduct in his earthly days.

Addressing the community members as "Beloved" in 2:7, as this writing will do again in 3:2, 21 and 4:1, 7, 11, 1 John reminds them that theirs is a traditional faith. The fellowship they already possess flees innovation. It is strongly intimated to them that there are others who do not hold fast to the "old commandment" of love for brothers and sisters, which they have had "from the beginning" (vv. 7b, 10a). Departers from this "word" that the writer has transmitted should know, as he knows, that Jesus called what was by now old among them "a new commandment" (v. 8a; cf. John 13:34). The writer is repudiating any interpretation of that new commandment that does not take literally what Jesus said: "Just as I have loved you, you also should love one another" (ibid.) and he knows that there are such interpreters abroad. The newness of Jesus' commandment does not consist in the replacement of law in the First Testament by love. Cain's murder of his brother will shortly be identified as a lack of brotherly love (1 John 3:11-12). No, what was new about it was its relation to the new covenant enunciated in 1 Corinthians 11:25 and Luke 22:20.

Jesus at the supper table foretold the renewal of the Mosaic covenant — which Jeremiah 31:31-34 had prophesied — in his blood. The new commandment of love of GJohn effects a fresh relation with God and a consequent intimacy among believers. It is made possible by Jesus' laying down his life for them in order to take it up again (see John 10:17b). Jeremiah had written of the new way God's covenant would be kept in the last times, namely, by the LORD's making the law interior to the people of Israel, "writing it on their hearts" (31:35b). Jesus spoke of just such a new law observance and new peoplehood. His disciples after his resurrection saw in him the inaugurator of the final age. For them the "new commandment" of the Johannine circle needed repeating as something "true [i.e., realized] in him and in you" (1 John 2:8a; cf. 2:27, the only other use of "true" in this letter). The adjective "true" in GJohn means "the only real." It is effected as such by God's revelation in Jesus the Son. Since "truth" is this revelation of God, it can be applied to anything Jesus does or says. It can also be applied to his followers who come after him if they walk in his way. The new commandment is true in them because "the darkness is passing away and the true light is already shining" (v. 8).

Obedience to the commandment by the 1 John community

makes real or true the commandment as new. It thereby causes
the darkness to pass away. The "true light," which is Christ and
all that he accomplishes, is already shining when this commandment is kept (v. 8c; cf. John 1:5, 9; 3:19; 8:12; 12:46). Contrasted
to it is the boast "I am in the light," when it is made by someone
who continues to hate a brother or a sister. Such a one is "still
in the darkness" (v. 9). (The technical term *adelphós*, meaning
a fellow believer, is used generically for both sexes and hence
is rightly translated "a brother or a sister.") What can this hatred be to which the epistle will again and again return (2:11;
3:15; 4:20)? How can those who harbor it be called "murderers"
(3:15)? In the writer's mind it is something more vicious than
simply thinking ill of others, which is quite bad enough. One
rightly suspects that the believers who are the object of this hatred by others are those who believe as 1 John does. If so, the
author has brought it out in the open that not keeping Christ's
commandments, walking in darkness, and declaring themselves
free of sin are characteristics of a party that, in its schism, hates
the brothers and sisters of the writer. Whether the opponents
are guilty of this hate or not, they are conceived by the author
as harboring it. Whatever the case, 1 John in making the charge
is not far from returning the compliment.

These mutual recriminations are a stumbling-block for modern Christians who like to think of their faith, especially its
Johannine expression, as purged of all hatred. Little relief is
provided by the thought that Christians over the ages have con-
sistently hated each other on ethnic and political, even religious
grounds, usually couched as perceived injustices of long stand-
ing. If it is true that two wrongs do not make a right, the proverb
should have special meaning for adherents to the gospel. But any
defense of first-century hatreds is bound to be weak. One exten-
uation of writings like GJohn and 1 John that has been tried is
the declaration that the community or communities that produced them knew they were being hated, respectively, by *hoi
Ioudaîoi* ("the super-Jews" who opposed the Johannine Jews) and
those who "went out from us" (1 John 2:19), but the communities did not respond in kind. There is little in the tenor of these
writings to sustain the view. The love among fellow believers

that the Gospel and the epistles do enjoin is highly edifying. There is in them, however, nothing like the love of enemies taught by Jesus in Matthew 5:43–48 and Luke 6:27–28.

What cannot be excused can at least be explained. First, it has taken Christians many centuries to learn to love their enemies. Even at that, those who have achieved it are very few. It is therefore unreasonable to expect the lesson to be mastered by any within a few decades of the Resurrection. Second, and more to the point, the Johannine circle had the same outlook as the Hebrew (later the Israelite, then the Jewish) people from whom they came and doubtless were. Like their religious predecessors they viewed their enemies as identical with the enemies of God. Those who "went out from us" of 2:19 had not simply formed another congregation once they experienced some new insights on the apostolic message. In their misconstrual of who Jesus is and what he does in God's plan (to be developed in 1 John 2–5), they have taken a stand against God. Their teaching is a deceit; hence it is in no sense to be tolerated. They *cannot* be loved because, doing the devil's work as they are, they are literally unlovable. An apt comparison would be the hatred various Christian groups have harbored for each other from the eleventh century onward or from the sixteenth century to the nineteenth, including the virulent anti-Catholicism that continues to this day. "Love your enemies" is understood by such hating Christians to describe one's personal enemies but not those theological opponents who are enemies of God. The writer of 1 John would have been revolted at the suggestion that the departers from the midst of his group could have been loved. They "hated the brethren" in the positions they had adopted on the Johannine tradition. Loving them would have been as much an impossibility as loving Satan and his works.

A believer living in the light loves fellow believers as a matter of course. There is in such a one no "cause for stumbling" (v. 10). The noun used here, *skándalon*, is a stone in the road that bruises the sandaled foot or sends a beast tumbling. Jesus says much the same thing using the cognate verb *skandalízein:* "I have said these things to you to keep you from stumbling" (John 16:1). The more familiar English word "scandalize" has ac-

quired too many trivial connotations to be serviceable in 1 John,
which is speaking of causing another's spiritual ruin. Hatred for
another believer is a sign of walking in the darkness, a darkness
that renders the hater blind (vv. 10–11). Beyond question those
who have seceded are considered guilty of this conduct and are
so charged. But could a member of the fellowship commit the
heinous crime of hating another member? The letter has already
allowed the possibility of sin by a believer (2:1), but the context
of this later part of the chapter, vv. 3–11, is quite different. It
concerns the hatred that the writer perceives toward his believers. Should any of them be guilty of it, they too would become
apostates, secessionists like the others.

Assurance Followed by Admonishment

2 **12**I am writing to you, little children
  because your sins are forgiven on account of his name.
 13I am writing to you, fathers,
  because you know him who is from the beginning.
 I am writing to you, young people,
  because you have conquered the evil one.
 14I write to you, children,
  because you know the Father.
 I write to you, fathers,
  because you know him who is from the beginning.
 I write to you, young people,
  because you are strong and the word of God abides
   in you,
 and you have overcome the evil one.

2 **15**Do not love the world or the things in the world. The love
of the Father is not in those who love the world; **16**for all that
is in the world — the desire of the flesh, the desire of the eyes,
the pride in riches — comes not from the Father but from the
world. **17**And the world and its desire are passing away, but
those who do the will of God live forever.

The harsh tone of the previous section, while directed against
those who are no longer of the writer's company, could well

intimidate those who are. To guard against any misinterpreta-
tion the writer adopts a gentler tone. He reminds his fellow
believers of their supremely advantaged condition. He may do
this to build them up for the stern warning he is about to deliver against love of the world (vv. 15–19). Or, again, the two
segments may not stand in such a relation. It has been noted frequently that the cohesiveness of 1:1–2:11 will not be repeated
after that point. The material that follows it is more a collec-
tion of warnings and exhortations, negative and positive, that
do not do much to advance the ideas found in the early part of
the letter.

The differences of address ("little children," v. 12; cf. 2:1;
"young people," vv. 13c, 14e; "children," v. 14a) and the alter-
nation of tenses of the verb "write" are probably stylistic, like
the words for "love" and "sheep" and "lambs" in GJohn 21:15–
17. No special significance should be attached to them beyond
the repetition of *teknía* (v. 12a; "little children") from 2:1a as
encompassing all in the one term of warmth. The addressees of
the five subsequent reasons the author finds for writing are the
young and the old in age or belief. Children may be intended by
paidía (v. 14) and young adults by *neaniskoi* (vv. 13, 14) but we
cannot be sure. What matters is that faithful believers in Christ
of a wide spread of ages — and *patéres* stands for both parents
just as *adelphoi* means male and female believers — are being
reminded of their spiritual blessings. All have had their sins forgiven through the "name," that is, the person, of Christ (v. 12).
They and the fathers (see v. 14d) have the knowledge of him who
is "from the beginning," here meaning the beginning of Jesus'
self-disclosure to his disciples rather than the timeless *archè* of
GJohn 1:1. Previously, knowledge had been of God (2:3a, 4a),
not Christ, but v. 13 presses home the point that the addressees
have true knowledge as contrasted with the knowledge claimed
by the opponents that is false. By their faith and baptism the
in-group have conquered the evil one (v. 13b). They know the
Father (v. 14b) even as they know Christ. They have been made
strong in him who was from the beginning and this has enabled
them to overcome the evil one (v. 14c, a repetition of v. 13b).
God's word abides in those (v. 14c) who can say, "I abide in

[God]" (v. 6). Because of their vigor in the struggle they can all, even the elderly, be addressed as youths.

The "world" of vv. 15–17 should not immediately be identified with the evil one of v. 14c, as those familiar with GJohn might be prone to do (see John 12:31, 14:30, 16:11). The world as such or as God's creation is not the problem, as a Marcionite reading would have it. The world can be, rather, a strong rival for the human affections that should be directed toward God (the "love of the Father" of v. 15 being an objective genitive, not God's love for us). Quite simply, the world is a dangerous place for its human inhabitants. The things of the world can draw us away from the God who made them. *Abusus non tollit usum* (Misuse does not nullify proper use), says the old watchword; but the ill use of possessions and learning and power has been a threat to their right use from time immemorial. If "the world" is a potential enemy to believers in this threefold exhortation, the "desire of the flesh" (v. 16) is surely another. In the Bible *bsr*, flesh, means humanity in all its limitation and weakness. It is by no means confined to the sex passion. It is, however, in Jewish writing contemporaneous with the Dead Sea Scrolls and the Sayings of the Fathers, related to sinful desire more than to resistance to temptation. "Flesh" may, of course, connote lust or sexual transgression, but it can equally refer to excess at the table, covetousness, or simple greed.

The third member, "the desire of the eyes" (ibid.), suggests the lustful gaze or any covetous glance, while "life" in "the pride of life" in sources contemporary with 1 John connotes roughly what is intended by "the good life" in today's parlance: the satisfaction taken in property and possessions, hence "the pride in riches" (NRSV). This brief catalogue of "all that is in the world" describes what originates from the world, not from the Father (see v. 16). The conclusion to the formidable array pitted against those who would live in the light is a reassuring, "Not to worry!" That is because transience marks the world made up of desires whereas "one who does God's will" (NRSV's "those" is singular in Greek) survives "to the end of the age." Whatever has to do with God abides, for God is permanent; all creaturehood is passing. The sentiment is not so much an expression of Jewish apocalyptic thought as it is a simple contrast between God and creatures, however alluring they may prove in the short run. Obeying God's commandments or word (see 2:3, 4, 5) is the same as "doing God's will" (v. 17). It provides the assurance of "living forever," a Johannine idea that is only occasionally related to judgment and the world to come. The phrase usually describes an abiding *now,* a present state of life in God.

THE MANY ANTICHRISTS:
DENIERS OF THE FATHER AND THE SON

2 [18]Children, it is the last hour! As you have heard that antichrist is coming, so now many antichrists have come. From this we know that it is the last hour. [19]They went out from us, but they did not belong to us; for if they had belonged to us, they would have remained with us. But by going out they made it plain that none of them belongs to us. [20]But you have been anointed by the Holy One and all of you have knowledge. [21]I write to you, not because you do not know the truth, but because you know it, and you know that no lie comes from the truth. [22]Who is the liar but the one who denies that Jesus is the Christ? This is the antichrist, the one who denies the Father and the Son. [23]No one who denies the Son has the Father; everyone who confesses the Son has the Father also. [24]Let what you heard from the beginning abide in you. If what you heard from the beginning abides in you, then you will abide in the Son and in the Father. [25]And this is what he has promised us, eternal life.

[26]I write these things to you concerning those who would deceive you. [27]As for you, the anointing that you received from him abides in you, and so you do not need anyone to teach you. But as his anointing teaches you about all things, and is true and is not a lie, and just as it has taught you, abide in him.

The address "Little children" (*teknía*) occurred in 2:1 and will again (v. 28). Its appearance in v. 18 as the warm *paidía* is thought by some to signal a new section. Schnackenburg, having identified 1:5–2:17 as Part One (after the prooemium of four verses) concludes that 2:18–3:24 form Part Two and 4:1–5:12 Part Three. He entitles them, respectively, "Fellowship with God Means Walking in the Light," "The Contemporary Situation of the Christian Communities," and "The Separation of Those Who Belong to God from the 'World,'" all three followed by a subtitle. If his division has merit, the situation of the communities as 1 John perceives it in Part Two is dire. His phrase "the last hour" is unique in the Bible, although terms like "the day," "the last day," and "the hour" proliferate. This writing looks forward to the end-time, like all the books of the First Testament, but as in Jewish eschatology generally no attempt is made to calculate the date of its arrival. It is simply a misconception of this type of futurist thinking to say that those who engaged in it foresaw the end as chronologically "imminent" or "soon." Time words are used, but they have no significance except as saying "future," "sudden," and "certain." Clearer is the fact that the writer views the departure of those "who did not belong to us" (v. 19) as a sign that the last hour—whatever it means—has arrived.

Did they leave of their own choice or were they ejected? If queried, would they have claimed that the 1 John community left them or had been dismissed by them? It is impossible to say other than that the writer speaks for one of two aggrieved parties, confident that the adversaries are in the wrong. In all schisms there is enough blame to share. This is not to say that nothing can be known of the causes of the present division. From the writer's point of view they are clear. Those who seceded did so because they did not know the truth (see v. 21). Their lie was the denial that Jesus is the Christ, that the Father and the Son are somehow not the common possession of believers.

The term "antichrist" occurs here for the first time in the Christian Scriptures. It lacks the article in both the singular and the plural. It will appear only in 1 John (2:18, 22; 4:3) and 2 John 7, in the last three cases with the article. The "lawless one...destined for destruction" of 2 Thessalonians 2:3–4 would seem to be this same mysterious adversary of Christ and the gospel. The identification of antichrist with Beliar (see 2 Cor.

6:15; an Aramaic name for Satan, God's adversary, in the Qumrân writings and the *Testaments of the Twelve Patriarchs* [second century B.C.E.]) is a development later than the First Testament. The term or concept "antichrist" is evidently older in the tradition than 1 John. The audience is already aware that such a one "is coming" (2:18), perhaps even as part of the message that "was heard from the beginning" (see 2:7, 24; 3:11). The Pauline author of 2 Thessalonians 2:3–4 deals with the precedence of the day of the Lord by the activity of the rebel deceiver as if it were a fact well known from the earliest preaching. In that passage an individual will "oppose and exalt himself above every so-called god or object of worship" (v. 4), a reference to Daniel 11:36. He will go so far as to "declare himself to be God" (v. 4).

Here in 1 John the expectation of antichrist as one to come has been realized in the "many antichrists who have come," namely, the seceders (2:18–19). The broadening out of a person or force set against God's Christ to a body of dissidents from true faith is found in this place only. True faith consists in affirming that Jesus is the Christ (v. 22) and that this "Jesus Christ has come in the flesh from God" (4:2). This is an expanded version of the cryptic proposition denied by the departers, "the Father and the Son" (2:22). The author of 1 John has made an application of an earlier Christian tradition to a situation of his own day. He is so convinced of the harm done by false teachers that he does not hesitate to identify them with the great opponent of God and Christ in the cosmic struggle of "the last hour" (v. 18).

The truth of Christ's coming from God in the flesh is something that "all of you know" (v. 20; "you know" repeated in v. 21). This knowledge came with "anointing" (*chrîsma*, v. 20) by the Holy One, an idea already found in 2 Corinthians 1:21: "It is God who establishes us with you in Christ and has anointed us." It is not immediately clear whether the Holy One is God or Christ. The verbal association of chrism and Christ and the "from him" and "his" of v. 27 seem to indicate that Christ is intended (see Mark 1:24, Luke 4:34, John 6:69, Acts 3:14, and Rev. 3:7 for references to him as the Holy One). Yet the title "Holy One of Israel" is frequent for God in the First Testament and is found with the article in the Septuagint. It could well be

that 1 John intends the ambiguity, attributing knowledge of the
relation between God and Christ to the figurative anointing of
coming to believe, or even the literal one of a rite at baptism.

If the anointing has conferred knowledge on "all of you"
(v. 20) and this knowledge encompasses "all things" without
"the need of anyone teaching you" (v. 27), it is somewhat puzzling that the Christhood of Jesus and the confession of the Son
as tantamount to "having the Father" should be specified so ve-
hemently. Undoubtedly, the reason is that there has been denial
of these points in the sense the author understands them and
in which he associates fellow members of the community with
himself. The differences must have been long and painful to account for the acrimonious hurling of the charge "antichrists."
They culminated the disputes within the ethnic Jewish John
community over true faith in Jesus (see GJohn 3:17–21; 8:31–
38). A substantial body has left the 1 John community over this
question and, from the epistle's standpoint, continues to try to
deceive it in the matter (2:26). The description of one who denies that Jesus is the Christ as "the liar" (v. 22) is an echo of the
devil as "a liar and the father of lies" (John 8:44). The Gospel
had attributed sonship of the devil to those who claim to be offspring of Abraham but do not have Johannine faith in Jesus. By
the time 1 John is written the schism is complete. They are gone
and the author wishes ill fortune to them.

A word of digression on the use of the term "antichrist"
in Christian polemic is in order here. The second- and third-
century fathers, interpreting the church's Scriptures, foresaw
the coming of this figure only after the fall of the Roman em-
pire. By the time of St. John of Damascus in the East and St. Bede
in the West (both seventh century), scriptural commentary on
the Thessalonian correspondence, Revelation, and the Johannine epistles had come to view the mentions of the antichrist
in a more general way as opposition to the gospel. The short,
sober *Libellus de Antichristo* of the French Benedictine abbot Adso
(d. 992), a figure revived by the fictional treatment given him in
Umberto Eco's *The Name of the Rose*, does not go beyond the
biblical data other than identifying him as the son of Dan of
Genesis 49:17. The prediction of the Cistercian abbot Joachim

of Fiore (twelfth century) that the antichrist would arise as a pseudo-pope, however, gave currency to the notion that 1 and 2 John had made a specific prophecy. After that the church and sometimes the Roman bishop became favorite candidates for the distinction at the hands of the Waldensians, Wyclif and the Lollards, various Bohemian reformers, and the Spiritual Franciscans. During the Crusades "the Turk" or "the Saracen" inherited the mantle. Various English miracle plays featured the Antichrist as a character, while William Langland (fourteenth century) in his *Vision of Piers Plowman* describes "the Coming of Antichrist" in detail as part of his prevailing hope for spiritual and social conversion.

From that point on various Protestant reformers, among them Tyndale, Luther, and Calvin, were convinced that the pope was the one spoken of in Scripture and that members of the Catholic or Roman Church were the seceders. William Tyndale's 1531 commentary on 1 John said that "antichrist...preached Christ wilily...and set up innumerable ceremonies, and sacraments, and imagery....The Bishop of Rome made a law of his own, to rule his church by, and put Christ's out of the way."

As sects proliferated, the Puritans were sure the bishops of the Church of England were the antichrist. Oliver Cromwell at one point received the designation by way of riposte from the Anglicans. Sir Isaac Newton was certain in his *Observations upon the Prophecies of Daniel and the Apocalypse of John* that the papacy was the antichrist. In the American colonies Benjamin Harris's *New England Primer* of 1737 included an illustration of "the Pope, or Man of Sin." Later Napoleon, Hitler, and Stalin were severally identified as the one prophesied. Across the ages, however, this menacing figure is most likely to be the pope because the incumbent of that pastoral office has more staying power than the peoples, sects, and tyrants mentioned above. (For an extended treatment of this question, one should consult W. Roger Williams's entry "Antichrist" in David Lyle Jeffrey, general editor, *A Dictionary of Biblical Tradition in English Literature* [Grand Rapids: William B. Eerdmans, 1992]).

Returning to the text at 2:24–27, we find that the plea, "let what you heard from the beginning abide in you," namely, the revelation concerning the word of life (see 1:1–2), comes closer in phrasing to GJohn than anything we have encountered so far. The word of Christ or of God is to remain in those who believe rightly. If it does, they will continue to dwell in the Son and in the Father (v. 24). This is very close to what is said in GJohn 14:11a, 23; 15:4a; 16:3, 27–28; 17:6–7, 24–26, as those passages stress the intimacy (later, "coinherence") of Father and Son and the promised abiding of believers in both. The passage peaks (2:25) in the term "eternal life," out of Daniel 12:2 (see John 3:16, 36; 5:24; cf. 6:47; 11:25–26). A difference is that in the Gospel this life is often but not always spoken of as a present possession, whereas in 1 John 2:25 it is the subject of a promise, *epaggelía*. Still, GJohn can speak of "the resurrection of life" as a future reality (5:29). The notion of futurity likewise appears in passages where "eternal life" occurs (see 4:14, 36; 6:27; 12:25). Since "what we will be has not yet been revealed" (1 John 3:2), eternal life in its fullness is unquestionably something that is promised in the present.

Abide as God's Children Now and Be Sure of Christ at His Coming

2 **28**And now, little children, abide in him, so that when he is revealed we may have confidence and not be put to shame before him at his coming. **29**If you know that he is righteous, you may be sure that everyone who does right has been born of him. 3 **1**See what love the Father has given us, that we should be called children of God; and that is what we are. The reason the world does not know us is that it did not know him. **2**Beloved, we are God's children now; what we shall be has not yet been revealed. What we do know is this: when he is revealed, we will be like him, for we will see him as he is. **3**And all who have this hope in him purify themselves, just as he is pure.

Even though the message heard from the beginning, sealed by baptismal anointing, continues to be a reality that dispenses with the need of further teaching (vv. 24–27), believers can still

be exhorted to perseverance. Such is the burden of these next
five verses. The one to be revealed in the future is the Christ
in glory at his "coming" (*parousía*, v. 28, the only occurrence
of the term in the Johannine corpus). This confirms that he is
the Holy One spoken of in v. 20. Failure to abide in him and
the shame that will follow are named as distinct possibilities.
Otherwise, believers would not have to be exhorted to lives that
will bring them before the judge with the "courage" (or better
"confidence" —*parrhēsía*) of a good conscience. Undoubtedly the
writer here shares the common view of early Christians that an
upright life (see v. 29) must be maintained to ensure salvation
at the time of one's appearance before Jesus as judge (see Acts
10:42; Matt. 25:31-46). Since he is known to be just (or righteous), he stands forth as the begetter of all who do what is right
(v. 29). They are "born of him" much as GJohn, in 3:3, speaks of
being born "from above." The thought that the upright pattern
their lives on the righteous Jesus Christ will be underscored in
1 John 3:7. Here it concludes the section on the assured reward
at Christ's coming of those who remain faithful to him, resisting
the appeal of those "who have gone out from us" (2:19).

At this point the author of the epistle wishes to underscore
the marvelous intimacy of abiding in the Son and in the Father.
It is no less than being made "children of God" by the gift of
the Father's love (3:1). This present reality will inevitably lead to
the estrangement of the world from those thus parented by God.
The echoes of GJohn are unmistakable: the power to become
children of God given to all who believe in the word who is the
true light (1:12) and the failure of the opponents of the Jesus
community to know "him who sent me." The epistle will shortly
tell believers that they should not be surprised by the world's
hatred (1 John 3:13; see GJohn 15:18-19, 23). "The world," usually a term for outsiders to the Johannine believers, cannot know
the community as the offspring of God because it has not known
God in intimate conjunction with the Son (see 1 John 3:1). This
relationship within deity — the divine becoming human in the
Son within time—serves as the pattern for the intimate relation
of believers with God.

The magnificence of the gift of God's love receives the stress here. The world knows nothing like it. But the present situation is only the beginning. At the parousia when God is revealed there will come to pass a unique human likeness to deity. The experience of God's love for believers is their present condition. That is what being God's children means. At Christ's coming this love will achieve the highest fruition the creature is capable of: a God-likeness that looking upon the face of God will bring about (see 3:2).

Is the writer presenting his readers with a quite new theology of future intimacy with God? It would seem not. His repeated use of "you know" and "we know" (see 2:21; 3:5, 15; 5:15) indicates a presumed familiarity with a teaching about the parousia already transmitted and received. 1 John is one long reminder of the tradition, put forward as a bastion against the false and deceitful teaching it perceives as a threat to the life of faith. The tradition is one of "hope" (*elpída*, 3:3, the only occurrence of this noun in Gospel and epistles). Brown observes that "only the Johannine stress on realized eschatology can explain the absence of such an important Christian theological theme" as hope in the Gospel (p. 396). Yet futurist eschatology is not a total absentee from GJohn, as witness 5:28–29, 11:23, and 12:48. It has been pointed out that references to realized eschatology in this Gospel always have a reference to the traditional Jewish hope of future vindication lurking nearby (see George MacRae, "The Fourth Gospel and *Religionsgeschichte*," *Catholic Biblical Quarterly* 32, no. 1 [January 1970], 18).

"Likeness to God and seeing God," as Schnackenburg notes, "together sum up the whole content of Christian hope. . . . In the shape of a categorical announcement the author states that those who have this hope purify themselves" (pp. 160, 161). Although its origins are in cultic practice (see John 2:6; 11:55), the verb "purify" has long since taken on an ethical meaning, as in the injunction, "Cleanse your hands, you sinners, and purify your hearts" (James 4:8), and, "Now that you have purified your souls by your obedience to the truth . . ." (1 Pet. 1:22). Just as Jesus Christ is a "pure" one (*hagnós*, 3:3) and "in him there is no sin" (v. 5), so those who hope in a future revelation of God must be pure "as he is." The purifying of the self spoken of in this verse is not a deed achieving self-righteousness; rather it is a further emulation of Jesus who said, "And for their sakes I sanctify myself, so that they also may be sanctified in truth" (John 19:19). The preparation for the self-disclosure of God at the end that is enjoined is a life of fidelity in sinlessness.

In closing, a few lines from the fifth-century B.C.E. Malachi should be noted. God as the Father-Creator of sons and daughters begins to appear in postexilic writings such as Deuteronomy 32:6 and Isaiah 43:6; 63:16, peaking perhaps in the anguished cry: "Have we not all one father? Has not one God created us? Why then are we faithless to one another, profaning the covenant of our ancestors?" (Mal. 2:10). More tender still is the earlier Hosean picture of God as a solicitous parent. It describes Israel as a beloved child, a son called out of Egypt. It was God who taught Ephraim to walk, healed it and led it, then took this people up into embrace "like those who lift infants to their cheeks. I bent down to them and fed them" (Hos. 11:1, 3–4). This is the biblical tenderness that prepares for God's chosen in Christ to be called — like all Israel — to be children of God now and unspeakably closer in a time to come.

RIGHTEOUSNESS MEANS THE AVOIDANCE OF SIN, WHICH MAKES CHILDREN OF THE DEVIL

3 **4**Everyone who commits sin is guilty of lawlessness: sin is lawlessness. **5**You know that he was revealed to take away sins, and in him there is no sin. **6**No one who abides in him sins; no one who sins has either seen him or known him. **7**Little children, let no one deceive you. Everyone who does what is right is righteous, just as he is righteous. **8**Everyone who commits sin is a child of the devil; for the devil has been sinning from the beginning. The Son of God was revealed for this purpose, to destroy the works of the devil. **9**Those who have been born of God do not sin, because God's seed abides in them; they cannot sin, because they have been born of God. **10**The children of God and the children of the devil are revealed in this way; all who do not do what is right are not from God, nor are those who do not love their brothers and sisters.

There is a certain repetitious quality to the earlier part of this passage. This should not surprise us in a writing that develops themes from GJohn. "Little children," "deceive," "doing right," "righteousness," "being born of God," and "children of God" have all appeared in the epistle in similar contexts. What is new is the emphasis on sin and sinfulness, although attributing it to the devil as its cause and sinners as his progeny is a clear echo of the Gospel (John 8:41a, 44a). These verses are censorious of those who are not children of God and quite certain that their choice of sin sets them in an opposition to the John people as sharp as that between God and the devil. The fact that this passage leads to the commandment to love one another (3:10) does nothing to relieve its harshness, neither does its identity of the Son of v. 8 as sinless or as revealed to take away our sins (v. 5). If anything, vv. 4 and 8 heighten the horror of sin.

The believers whom the epistle addresses as little children are the ones to whom this grim passage is directed. "Lawlessness" is the literal translation of *anomía,* but in this context the writer does not seem to have departure from divine or human positive precept in mind. He envisions, rather, sheer unadulterated evil. Later it will be called "wrongdoing" in the NRSV (*adikía,* 5:17) but this rendering scarcely covers the rebellion against God connoted by the Septuagintal term. While the Judaism of the time knew no dualism of a metaphysical sort, it did not hesitate to limn the devil and his works as the polar opposite to the all-holy God. The Johannine Christian can and must renounce sin, understood here as lawless, wicked behavior. Lesser offenses are simply not in question.

Very early, 1 John admitted the tragic possibility that a believer in Christ could sin. Deniers of such a possibility were castigated as self-deceived (see 1:8, 10; cf. 2:1). But this passage says: "Those who have been born of God . . . cannot sin, because they have been born of God" (3:9). The contradiction here requires exploring. To begin, we observe the diametric opposition between Christ and sin assumed in these lines. In him who was revealed as one sent by God to take away sins there is no sin (v. 5; cf. John 8:46). No one who sins can *have* seen him or known him (v. 6). The claim of the writer, however, is that he and his fel-

low believers *have* seen him (1:1), *have* known him if they have
kept his commandments (2:3–4). Does the author, then, make
the claim that he is beyond the power of sin? Verse 9 says clearly
that he and those like him do not and cannot sin.

Raymond E. Brown is certainly right in saying, "No matter what the author thought, the wording of his affirmations
about sinlessness and impeccability is not sufficiently nuanced"
(p. 430). Every sort of resolution of the difficulty has been
proposed, from the theory that author and editor were two different persons to the elite versus ordinary Christians theory
and its cognate, which holds that grievous versus more readily
forgivable sins are in question. Brown quotes St. Augustine as
providing the commonest held view, which nonetheless does not
remove the contradiction: "To the extent that the Christian remains in Christ, to that extent he does not sin" (*On the Epistle*
4.8; *Sources Chrétiennes* 75, 234). Given the diametric opposition
between the holiness of Christ and the disobedience to God that
is sin, Augustine's statement is axiomatic. A person is either in
one condition or the other, a friend to Christ or his enemy and
thus a "child of the devil" (v. 8).

The acknowledgment that this epistle is self-contradictory, at
least by force of words, is abhorrent to those who are convinced
that the Spirit of truth cannot permit such a lapse. Of these, a
number have over the centuries taken the position of the ab-
solute impeccability of those who have once come to justifying
faith. Any who do sin are not, in this view, guilty of apostasy but
simply prove that theirs had not been the faith that saves in the
first place. The view that uninterrupted moral perfection characterizes the life of the "saved" is a great vote of confidence in
the grace of God. It is based on a definition of what being saved
means, namely, the inability to sin. The argument is circular and,
as such, incontrovertible. The texts of the New Testament and
even of this epistle go in the other direction, however. They say
that, tragically, the person in grace can fall.

The reason given for the fact that those born of God (v. 9;
cf. GJohn 3:3–6; 5:1, 4) do not sin is that "God's seed abides
in them" (v. 9; cf. 2:29, 3:1–2). We have to move ahead to 3:24
and 4:13 to see that "seed" is here a metaphor for the Spirit

that Christ in the first instance and God in the second has given us. Irenaeus, Hippolytus, and Clement of Alexandria, in the concluding years of the second century and first half of the third, all assure us that the divine "seed" characterizes the true gnostic in their writings. In the gnostic understanding it is at the core of the pneumatic or spiritual person. That thought system is also deeply committed to the idea of divine begetting. The similarities of word use bring to the surface the question of whether GJohn influenced the later development of Christian gnosticism or was influenced by proto-gnostic thought. Arguments in favor of the former are the stronger, although the unmistakable anti-gnostic, i.e., pro-matter, tone of 1 John (see 1:1, 2:2, 3:17, 4:2) creates the suspicion that the seed language may have been adopted to counter the incipient gnostic claim. The divine principle implanted in each believer is none other than a likeness to God that came with the gift of the Spirit. Being born of God, becoming children of God, was the result of the planting of this metaphorical seed.

Concerning the seven verses immediately preceding, a legitimate difficulty is this: does the sin or lawlessness so implacably argued against mean all moral wrongdoing or only the denial that Jesus is the Christ come in the flesh? That denial has caused secession or ejection from the GJohn community, which gives evidence of being identical with the 1 John community. Some commentators on the epistle see in it a sustained polemic against the seceders that is happy to find them guilty of every ethical offense, following in the train of their original departure from doctrinal truth. It seems more probable that their "not doing what is right" (*mḕ poiõn dikaiosýnēn*, 3:10) is an overall decline from the path of moral uprightness. Disobedience to God's commandments (see 5:2–3), failure to succor a brother or sister in need (3:17), succumbing to the lure of all that is in the world (2:16), constitute a fairly broad range of moral lapses. They may all exist in the mind of the writer. They surely follow from the initial sin in the order of deficient faith. But the sin seems cumulative or global in the mind of 1 John. It does not consist solely in the first decline down the slippery slope, their anti-incarnational stance, which equivalently denies the Father as well as the Son.

Murder and Hatred the Opposites of Mutual Love

3 **11**For this is the message you have heard from the beginning, that we should love one another. **12**We must not be like Cain who was from the evil one and murdered his brother. **13**Do not be astonished, brothers and sisters, that the world hates you. **14**We know that we have passed from death to life because we love one another. Whoever does not love abides in death. **15**All who hate a brother or sister are murderers, and you know that murderers do not have eternal life abiding in them. **16**We know love by this, that he laid down his life for us — and we ought to lay down our lives for one another. **17**How does God's love abide in anyone who has the world's goods and sees a brother or sister in need and yet refuses to help?

18Little children, let us love, not in word or speech, but in truth and action. **19**And by this we will know that we are from the truth and will reassure our hearts before him **20**whenever our hearts condemn us; for God is greater than our hearts, and he knows everything.

Raymond E. Brown favors 3:11 as the beginning of Part Two in a two-part division of the epistle. It begins, "This is the message," as does 1:5. This division yields two roughly equal parts, 1:5–3:10 and 3:11–5:12. The message or commandment to love one another (v. 11) will dominate this second part, as it does GJohn. It has already been enunciated in terms of the light-darkness antithesis in 2:7–11. This love is something believers have been taught from their first acquaintance with the gospel. Fellow believers are the primary objects of this love but others are not to be thought of as excluded. The fratricide of Cain — the only time this epistle makes an explicit biblical reference — is proposed as a horrible example. It is intended not only to dissuade from hatreds within the community but to explain the world's hatred for it (v. 13; "world" here in the hostile, GJohn sense). Genesis does not attribute the crime to the promptings of the evil one as 1 John does (v. 12) nor give any reason why God should have had regard for Abel's offering and none for Cain's (Gen. 4:5). We may speculate that the biblical author is expressing a preference for grazing over farming at the dawn of history (v. 2), but there does not seem to be compelling evidence for this. It may just be the mystery of God's choice as in the Isaac and Ishmael or Jacob and Esau stories. In any case, Cain's fiery response leading to murder is 1 John's example of where hatreds within the community may end. A few decades ago the example might have seemed extreme to our culture, but the current, terrifying proliferation of murder, even within families, makes it thoroughly apt. Persons totally out of control of their emotional lives who take a gun or a knife to settle a domestic score are a tragic commonplace.

There are only two conditions open to this writer as he proposes a familiar Semitic disjunction: abiding in death or in life, a life that for him is the divine life he calls "eternal" (*aiónion*, v. 15). Jesus' swift move from describing an angry word to the taking of a life in Matthew 5:21–22 is an indication of the hot-blooded culture in which both he and this later disciple lived. This follower never has Jesus far from his thoughts, even though he has not referred to him since 2:29. Now he speaks of his life given in sacrifice for our sakes in wording close to John 15:13 (v. 16a). He takes things further by proposing the fittingness of our doing likewise on one another's behalf (v. 16b). Deploring the callous unconcern for others in need (v. 17) comes close to the wording of James 2:15–16. This shows that deeds as the sole proof of love were as usual in Christian communities as in Judaism. "The world's goods" are again *bíos*, the "riches" or good life of 2:16; the refusal of "help" is *splánchna*, compassion or the "bowels of mercy" of KJV. The exhortation to show love by works (*en érgǭ*, v. 18), not by words, is strongly reminiscent of James 1:25 and 2:14–17. Acting "in truth" means sincerely but "from the truth" uses *aletheía* in another way — more in the manner of GJohn: namely, to describe acts that have their origin in God (see John 8:47b).

Verses 19b–20a provide a great problem for interpreters because they contain Greek phrasing unusual to this writer. There is also the uncertainty of the meaning of the verb that the NRSV translates "reassure." The probable meaning is that showing the truth of our love in deeds should calm our fears over whatever our heart might condemn us with. Conscience is thus set at rest by the knowledge that we have fulfilled love's demands.

The writer wishes, above all, to provide encouragement when a gnawing fear suggests to believers that they have not done enough (see 2:12–14). The all-knowing God is immense in mercy and can close any gap of inadequate human performance. "God is greater than our hearts" is the golden biblical text both to calm the scrupulous and to allay the fears of those who know they have come up short.

The Commandment Is to Believe in Christ and Love One Another

3 [21]Beloved, if our hearts do not condemn us, we have boldness before God; [22]and we receive from him whatever we ask, because we obey his commandments and do what pleases him. [23]And this is the commandment, that we should believe in the name of his Son Jesus Christ and love one another, just as he commanded us.

[24]All who obey his commandments abide in him, and he abides in them. And by this we know that he abides in us, by the Spirit he has given us.

The condition proposed in 3:20a was: "If our hearts condemn us" (Brown prefers the more literal, "know something prejudicial"). It was responded to by an assurance of the wideness of God's mercy. Verse 21a poses the opposite hypothesis: "If our hearts do not condemn us." Given that condition, we can certainly act with boldness (*parrhēsían*) before God. Awareness of our will to obey God with a view to pleasing God makes such boldness of action possible. Obeying the commandments or word of Christ (2:3–5) and loving a brother or sister (v. 10) have already been insisted upon, as has confessing the Son and the Father so as to abide in them (vv. 23, 24). Now these ideas are brought together under the double ensign of belief and the gift of the Spirit (v. 24). In the verb form "believe" this is the first time a favorite word of GJohn has occurred (v. 23). The consolidation of the two ideas is welcome. These concluding verses of chapter 3 package nicely the elements of faith, mutual love, obedience to Christ's commandments, and the mutual abiding of Christ and believers in him. The summary is repetitive but, then, all good summaries are.

Not yet mentioned but scarcely to be passed over is the assurance that we shall receive from God whatever we ask (v. 22). Jesus promised it in Matthew 7:7–8 and 18:19, and even more strongly in 11:24. The places to look for it in GJohn are 14:13–14 ("Anything you ask in my name I will do") and the more cryptic 16:26–27. There, Jesus says that no intercession by him will be needed. God already loves the disciples because they love him and believe that he came from the Father. Here in 1 John as in the Gospel occurrences, obedience to God's will is made the condition of receiving from God whatever we ask. People who storm heaven, only to be refused what they ask, need not deduce from this that there has been some flaw in their pleasing God that they are unaware of. The same is true of the current confusion of some biblical literalists who accuse others suffering from incurable illnesses of not having sufficient faith. The most reasonable and faith-filled response to texts like 3:22, "And we receive from [God] whatever we ask, because we obey his commandments and do what pleases him," is "What I asked for is evidently not God's will in the matter." That qualification, found in 5:14 below, is of supreme importance and should never be forgotten.

Discernment between True and False Spirits Dependent on Right Faith

4 ¹Beloved, do not believe every spirit, but test the spirits to see whether they are from God; for many false prophets have gone out into the world. ²By this you know the Spirit of God: every spirit that confesses that Jesus Christ has come in the flesh is from God, ³and every spirit that does not confess Jesus is not from God. And this is the spirit of the antichrist, of which you have heard that it is coming; and now it is already in the world.

⁴Little children, you are from God, and have conquered them; for the one who is in you is greater than the one who is in the world. ⁵They are from the world; therefore what they

say is from the world, and the world listens to them. **⁶**We are from God. Whoever knows God listens to us, and whoever is not from God does not listen to us. From this we know the spirit of truth and the spirit of error.

The gift of God's Spirit (1 John 4:2) has already occurred as a phrase in 3:24 and will again in 4:13 and 5:6–7. This gift provides an assurance that Jesus Christ abides in us and we in him. Its purpose, therefore, is truthful testimony, not the bestowal of multiple charisms as in other writings like Acts (2:4; 14:10) and the Pauline corpus (1 Cor. 12:4–11). If 1 John is being faithful to GJohn here, as is likely, that gift of Spirit was first given with water (see John 3:5–6) and makes possible the belief in the Son of Man that brings eternal life (vv. 15–16). The metaphors of anointing (2:20, 27) and God's seed (3:9) as abiding in those born of God are probably baptismal references, supposing that the thrust of the Nicodemus exchange of John 3 is toward the sacramental sign of new life. Is this "Spirit," which editors of translations put in upper case (the earliest codices are all in capital letters), deity itself, or is it a figure depicting begetting as a child of God? Or, again, is this spirit only one among the created spirits, good and bad, that populated Second Temple Judaism and have such a prominent place in its writings? The capitalization technique tells where the translators stand. Are they influenced by later developments in trinitarian theology? An examination of the first six verses of chapter 4 should provide an answer.

Up until now there has been ample warning against false teachers ("antichrists"; see 2:18–27). Beyond doubt the writer is afraid that some in his community will fall victim to their arguments, despite his assurance that the anointing they have received has provided them all with knowledge (vv. 20, 27). The fact that some have seceded is reason enough for him to be anxious. Hence this return to the dangers of deception in the most serious of matters, with a few criteria to assist in distinguishing truth from error. A long section on God as love and the effects of that love will follow (4:7–5:4), to be concluded by the power of right faith (5:5–12).

The false prophets are "many" (4:1; cf. 2:18). They are also human, although they may be diabolically impelled. Their offense is not a claim to superior knowledge or gifts, like the boastful behavior that St. Paul says some in Corinth have been given the gift to discern (1 Cor. 12:10). It is more like his putting the Thessalonians on guard with the same verb of admonition so that they will cleave to the good and abjure the evil (1 Thess. 5:21). The prophets 1 John warns against are simply wrong in what they teach. Are the spirits who are leading the faithful astray the deceitful spirits or demons of 1 Timothy 4:1? Perhaps, but in 1 John the teachers themselves are those spirits, just as the opposing good spirits who are "from God" have the teaching of Jesus' origins from God and incarnate status straight (v. 2). Human spirits are the ones making the true or false profession of faith. Distinguishing between them, between the Christ and the antichrist party, is a means to "know the Spirit of God" (4:2) who is clearly none of those human spirits. Every use of the term in this writing hypostatizes this Spirit, that is, makes it personal. It is not a characteristic or power of God or God merely in relation. The word designates a divine hypostasis or actor. This Spirit both enables believers to hold the confession, as Schnackenburg puts it, and "conversely it is the Spirit that is validated by that confession" (p. 200).

Jesus' coming in the flesh (v. 2) is important to the Johannine author; likewise his coming from God (ibid.). But as v. 10 will make clear, the reason for God's sending him is the matter of supreme importance. 1 John is not simply an anti-docetic tract or a Christ as truly divine tract. Its importance lies in its insistence on the soteriology that is the reason for the incarnation. The grievous error of the false prophets is their teaching that salvation comes some other way or from some other source. Without the subsequent progress of gnosticism in second-century Christianity we might not be able to learn the errors against which some of this epistle's dire warnings are directed.

The Coptic Nag Hammadi texts discovered in 1945, even more than the patristic citations from the writings that were found in those codices, put beyond doubt the view that the monastic compilers had of Johannine soteriology. They saw in all the writings of the John circle an influence of divine Spirit on the human spirit that required no mediation of the body or flesh or the cross. For them a heavenly Christ accomplished the deliverance of the human spirit from gross matter. Except as the teacher of a higher way no earthly Jesus was needed, least of all one "sent to be an atoning sacrifice for our sins" (1 John 4:10). Knowledge of the eons that proliferated in the heavens was the key to being set free from the captivity of the body and being transported above. There, one might expect to see a resolution of all contradiction and absorption into the All. The Johannine letters do not provide evidence that any such development has been achieved. They indicate only what the antichrist prophets are denying. The teaching attributed to these prophets, however, tends in a gnostic direction.

The "little children" who receive true teaching are told once again that they are from God and have vanquished the deceivers (4:4; cf. 2:20–21, 27). This is not their own doing but the work in them of one who is greater (*meízōn,* v. 4; cf. 3:20) than the one who is in the world. This latter has to be Satan or the evil one if GJohn is the epistle's main point of reference. In the Gospel he is three times called "the ruler of this [or the] world" (*árchōn;* John 12:31, 14:30, 16:11). If Christ and the spirits that confess him are from God, the deceiving spirits are from the world, which gives them willing audience (cf. 1 John 2:15–17). The "we" who are from God (v. 6) are not only proclaimers of the truth like the writer but also include all who adhere to it. Not unlike two armies set in battle array against one another, those who listen to the Johannine community and to the seceders from it are diametrically opposed. One party knows the spirit of truth, and hence is perfectly at ease in attributing to the other its being influenced by the spirit of error. "Error" (*plánē*) here is not just being wrong. From the Dead Sea Scrolls, the *Testaments of the Twelve Patriarchs,* and the Gospels and epistles (Matt. 27:64, Eph. 4:14, 2 Pet. 2:18, 3:17) we know that it connotes deception and falsehood. Satan and his minions invite to apostasy and spiritual ruin. Such is the work of the evil one, the lover of darkness and father of lies. Those who are not from God do not listen to "us" but to purveyors of "error" in that worst sense.

THE PROOF OF GOD'S LOVE FOR US:
AN ATONING SACRIFICE FOR SINS

4 ⁷Beloved, let us love one another, because love is from
God; everyone who loves is born of God and knows God.
⁸Whoever does not love does not know God, for God is love.
⁹God's love is revealed among us in this way: God sent his
only Son into the world so that we might live through him. ¹⁰In
this is love, not that we loved God but that he loved us and
sent his Son to be the atoning sacrifice for our sins. ¹¹Beloved,
since God loved us so much, we also ought to love one another. ¹²No one has ever seen God; if we love one another,
God lives in us, and his love is perfected in us.

1 John 3:1 has already stated that God has given us the love
that makes us God's children. Mutual love is exhorted to in 4:7,
but it has been described in 3:13 as the already existing fact. This
love that is from God makes possible being born of God and
knowing God. The loveless cannot know God, for God is love.
There is a connaturality between the capacity to love and knowing the one who is all love. These statements, although circular
in form, make clear that the love of believers for one another
and for God are all of a piece. It is God who makes both possible
and is the reason no one can have one without the other.

We are brought up short by professedly religious people who
constantly talk love but who have an enemies list. It sometimes
includes people very close to them by ties of blood or proximity.
Their rationalization is familiar: these are enemies of God; how
therefore *can* they be loved? More simply, in a religious frame-
work they are not "Christians" by the speakers' definition, which
means that there is no biblical injunction to include them in the
circle of love. This touches on an important exegetical point. Unquestionably 1 John, like the Qumrân literature and even GJohn,
is a community document. Does it anywhere enjoin the love of
all humanity or can it be seen to be restrictive — even exclusive
to the community — in its concerns?

One answer might be that *agápē* is by definition other-
regarding love. If it originates with the Infinite, who by nature
is love and nothing but love, then once received as a gift it can-

not be restricted. *Bonum est diffusivum sui* (Good is diffusive of itself), as an ancient philosophical axiom puts it. If the good tends by nature to be self-diffused, being otherwise incapable of action, how much more that good which is God-authored and God-directed. Note that "God is love" is a definition of deity (4:8a). The converse, love is God, is found nowhere in the Bible or in the Christian tradition. There have always been some who wished to apotheosize human love, but it cannot be done. The love that originates with us can be an intimation of God, can lead to God, but it must come from God if it is to be love in its fullness. That is because God is love.

In spite of the bold and unqualified declaration of v. 8, 1 John seems to say that only those who have been empowered to love on certain terms and to love certain people are capable of loving. Does the Jew not love, or the Muslim, or the Hindu? The suggestion is monstrous. And of course the seriously agnostic or atheist (not those who are casually such because they are too lazy to think), what of them? Obviously this ancient author has in mind only his fellow religionists and their opponents. You do not turn to him for an answer to a question far from his purview. But he has provided a few clues to *our* question.

If love is from God, one ought not attach restraints to it. 1 John indicates what those restraints or limits are: the desire of the flesh, the desire of the eyes, the pride in riches; callous disregard of those in need; yielding consciously to works of the devil, to sin. Many a person who is not a Christian, who has never heard of Jesus or of God as triune — or perhaps has heard of one or the other but always in terms of contempt — has done nothing but the works of love from early youth. Conversely, many who claim to know God fail the John test, which is actually the Jesus test (see Matt. 25:31–46). But, it may be pointed out, there is no love of enemies promulgated or so much as mentioned in this writing. What of that? To this the only effective response is that isolating a certain Scripture and cleaving to it without regard to all the others is what makes heretics. The Christian who is catholic — in the sense of universal or all-encompassing — accepts the whole revealed deliverance. In its fullness it teaches that the love that is from God takes in those who persecute and revile you.

Back to the letter. It seems to repudiate love *for* God (4:10a) but in fact this is so only if God's initiatory love is disregarded (10b). In this verse 1 John once again calls the Son a *hilasmós* (cf. 2:2), an "atoning sacrifice for our sins." The effect is expiatory: our sins are forgiven. The only fitting response to such an expression of love is love for one another (v. 11). "No one has ever seen God" (v. 12) bursts on us unexpectedly until we recall that GJohn employs it or something like it in three places where the superiority of Jesus to Moses and Elijah is being affirmed (1:18, 5:37, 6:46). This passage imitates the Gospel, although using a different verb from the one in those places and in 4:20 below. The point that God cannot be seen is conceded, only to be followed by an "if" that is better translated "but if." Mutual love of the same kind as that expressed by Jesus' sacrifice will make God an abiding presence within us. It will bring the divine love to perfection. God's love can be thought of as imperfect only from our side. What God does is done perfectly.

4 **13**By this we know that we abide in him and he in us, because he has given us of his Spirit. **14**And we have seen and do testify that the Father has sent his Son as the Savior of the world. **15**God abides in those who confess that Jesus is the Son of God, and they abide in God. **16**So we have known and believe the love that God has for us.

God is love, and those who abide in love abide in God and God abides in them. **17**Love has been perfected among us in this: that we may have boldness on the day of judgment, because as he is, so are we in this world. **18**There is no fear in love, but perfect love casts out fear; for fear has to do with punishment, and whoever fears has not reached perfection in love. **19**We love because he first loved us. **20**Those who say, "I love God," and hate their brothers or sisters, are liars; for those who do not love a brother or sister whom they have seen, cannot love God whom they have not seen. **21**The commandment we have from him is this: those who love God must love their brothers and sisters also.

5 **1**Everyone who believes that Jesus is the Christ has been born of God, and everyone who loves the parent loves the child.

²By this we know that we love the children of God, when we love God and obey his commandments.

In what has gone immediately before, the author has proposed God's love, which has taken the form of giving the Son in atoning death, as the model of human love. That theme is here continued. Verse 13 seems to be an interruption of it, however, until we observe its near identity with 3:24b. This makes it look like a formula that the author knows from the tradition and seems constrained to insert. His preferred teaching is that we abide in God but, yes, God has given us of the Spirit, as all believers know. This partaking of God's Spirit he places in the context of abiding in God. The deed of God that saves us is never far from the author's mind, and so he inserts it (vv. 14–15) in a near repetition of vv. 9–10. The description of Jesus as "Savior of the world" has appeared in only one other place in this Testament, namely, GJohn 4:42, where it is attributed to the villagers of Samaria expressing their new-found faith in Jesus. The abiding of God within is confined to those who can make this Johannine profession of faith.

After this brief digression the epistle returns to its consideration of the love God has for us (v. 16a). Verse 16b spells out luminously what has been said in vv. 8b and 13a. It is a packaged watchword for the Christian ages, combining a statement on God's very being as love and dwelling in love as tantamount to dwelling in God. Many of our contemporaries carry in their heads the haunting melody of African-American composer Clarence Rivers that has this verse as its refrain. "God is lo-o-ove, and those who abide in love abide in Go-o-od, and God in them." Some who are new to the refrain find themselves singing, "and those who abide in God abide in love." It makes no difference. If God is love the two can here be taken as interchangeable.

The perfection of love among us that has been spoken of in v. 12 is here defined (4:17). It is the "boldness" of 3:21 (and the NRSV's "confidence" in 2:28) that will mark our facing final judgment, the culmination of the "last hour" of 2:18. We have cause to be bold if "we are in this world" as he is. The "he" may be

God, with our actions in this life assumed to be God-like, but the antecedent is more likely to be the Son as Savior (vv. 14–15), specifically as offered to God in sacrifice (v. 10). Since the heavenly Christ is none other than the earthly Jesus he continues to be the model for our actions, even though we will have to face him as judge.

The biblical "fear of the LORD" is a sense of awe before the divine majesty, not craven fear. Nonetheless, the end-time teaching that marked Israel in the Second Temple period (the roots of "early Judaism") instilled a salutary fear in all who faced the judgment of the last day. It will be "a day of wrath, a day of wasting and of misery" (Zeph. 1:14–15). The phrase still rings in the present writer's ear from youthful service at many Christian funerals: "when Thou shalt come to judge the world by fire" (1 Cor. 3:13). This is the end-time fear v. 18 has in mind, referring to the day of judgment of the preceding verse. While punishment is to be feared the prospect of it is alien to those among whom love has been made perfect. Any residual fears of the last day prove that perfect love has not yet been achieved; it still must be. The two, fear and love, are totally incommensurate. One banishes the other (v. 18).

The Pauline admonition to "work out [pl.] your own salvation with fear and trembling" is as salutary today as in the days of lively end-expectation when the apostle penned it (Phil. 2:12). The complete disjunction 1 John makes between fear and love is not negated by this warning. An element of fear of the just judgment that Christ will render remains because Christians know in their hearts that their love has not been perfect. The sentiments of believers on this question have oscillated over the ages. First was the complete confidence in the saving power of God that marked the patristic era, then a fear of hell bordering on the paranoid in the early and late Middle Ages in the West, and now the modern conviction that hell simply cannot be in prospect for anyone. The latter takes its rise from two opposite sources: that the justifying faith Romans and Galatians speak of encompasses a perfect love and, second that God (if there be one) could not possibly condemn anyone, however evil, to such cruel torment. But most Christians fall into neither category. Whether they know the Bible at first hand or not, they instinctively know that perfect love casts out fear and that they must work out their salvation in fear and trembling.

God always makes the first move in the game of love (see v. 19). Whoever can say in response, in good conscience, "I love God" — it is the same test as "I am in the light" of 2:9 — must ask themselves how they fare in loving the *adelphós*. The NRSV makes the one who reflects on the question and the "brother" who is the object of the reflection plural for reasons of sexist sensitivity. The brother, now "brothers or [and] sisters," is, of course, not a sibling but a fellow believer. Facing the question we have encountered before, we know the term to be restricted to those who have the faith of the John community. For most of the centuries it would not have occurred to Christians to include the Jew, the Muslim or the heathen in that category, nor to them to include the Christian. Only with the enlargement of religious horizons of very recent date did it occur to followers of Jesus that all humanity is brother and sister to them in the John sense, although the stirrings of demand made by a nature common to all came earlier to the enlightened among all believers in God. In the present age most Christians would say that the Johannine love command extends to all without restriction. If pressed, however, they might acknowledge that fellow believers have a prior claim on their love.

The demand that love for the person who is seen be expressed in action as the sole proof of love for the unseen God (4:20) makes specific what has been said in 3:17. It also remarkably resembles James 2:14–15. This is not new teaching. All Israel had lived by it as it applied to fellow Jews and aliens in their midst, a similarly restrictive understanding. There are no religious peoples who think otherwise about how to serve — not many say "love" — the unseen God or gods. The chapter ends with an unequivocal statement of the necessary correspondence, even the convertible nature, of the love of God and of others (v. 21). It is not a suggestion delivered from on high. It is a divine command.

Belief, meaning right faith in Jesus' messiahship, brings about birth from God in 5:1. In 4:7 it had been mutual love. The parent and child reference of 5:1a is a way of saying that it would go against nature to claim love for God but not God's offspring (*tékna*, "children," 5:2). Obeying God's commandments is proof by our deeds of embracing the whole family, the divine and the divinized, in love.

Loving God Is Not Hard

5 ³For the love of God is this, that we obey his commandments. And his commandments are not burdensome, ⁴for whatever is born of God conquers the world. And this is the victory that conquers the world, our faith. ⁵Who is it that conquers the world but the one who believes that Jesus is the Son of God?

Victory and conquering are, of course, closely cognate words in Greek. One cannot read this short passage without being reminded of Jesus' *lógion*, "But take courage; I have conquered/ overcome the world!" (John 16:33c). The context in the Gospel is the disciples' promised victory over persecution, in which they will be at peace in the knowledge that Jesus has the Father with him. Here those who are God-begotten, acting on their faith in who Jesus is and what he does, are the victors. Once again, faith and love are seen as inseparable. St. Paul said in Galatians 5:6, as part of his insistence that circumcision was not necessary for that pagan population nor the absence of it any virtue in them: "The only thing that counts is faith working through love." It probably had been said both well and often before Paul inscribed it memorably. This is, in any case, 1 John's all but last word. His last word — an epilogue aside — is about testimony concerning the Son of God.

The True Faith That Conquers the World Relies on Testimony

5 ⁶This is the one who came by water and blood, Jesus Christ, not with the water only but with the water and the blood. And the Spirit is the one that testifies, for the Spirit is the truth. ⁷There are three that testify: ⁸the Spirit and the water and the blood, and these three agree. ⁹If we receive human testimony,

the testimony of God is greater; for this is the testimony of God that he has testified to his Son. **¹⁰**Those who believe in the Son of God have the testimony in their hearts. Those who do not believe in God have made him a liar by not believing in the testimony that God has given concerning his Son. **¹¹**And this is the testimony: God gave us eternal life, and this life is in his Son. **¹²**Whoever has the Son has life; whoever does not have the Son of God does not have life.

Jesus, the Son of God of 5:5 is, of course, the "one who came" of v. 6. "Jesus Christ," the name followed by the title without the intervening article, has appeared before this (1:3, 2:1, 3:23, 4:2), but not with the demonstrative pronoun "this" (*houtós*) as here. A special solemnity is indicated. It signals the formula "who came by water and blood," which is repeated for emphasis, "not with the water only but with the water and the blood" (v. 6). Who is it that would deny blood to Jesus Christ but concede water to him? Any who were ill at ease with his human fleshliness, the more especially with his having shed his blood on the cross. The gnostic-inclined could stomach pure, clear water, hence perhaps baptism as the rite Jesus underwent, but not the outpouring of his blood in death, least of all a eucharistic meal in which his blood was symbolically (i.e., sacramentally) drunk. This speculation would be baseless were it not for the numerous veiled allusions to baptism already made in the letter and the two overt references to Jesus as a *hilasmós* ("atoning sacrifice") for our sins. One affirms a thing as strongly as is done in v. 6 only if it has a history of being denied.

Having made the point of how Jesus Christ "came," probably on his saving mission, the author summons a witness. This is a technique employed throughout GJohn. The Spirit thus called has the designation "Spirit of truth" in the Gospel (John 14:17, 15:26, cf. 16:13). 1 John affirms with a characteristic boldness that "the Spirit *is* the truth" (v. 6). The subject of his testimony is that Jesus Christ came "by" (*en*) blood as well as water. The reference that comes to mind immediately is John 19:34, in which blood and water flow from the side of Jesus in his dying. The obvious target for the strong affirmation contained in this verse, which is moreover Spirit-attested, is a Christian party or group that will have none of it. If theirs is not an outright denial, they may be stressing Jesus' baptism over his death as the effective sign of his saving action. Their conviction that the Spirit was released at the baptism of believers, like the dove of the Gospel accounts, would be a further reason for 1 John to name the Spirit as testifying to the blood and not only water. Salvation is by Jesus' death, the epistle maintains. Anyone who denies this does not accept the witness of the truth-giving Spirit. Abstention from the Eucharist may be the practice under fire (see Ignatius, *To the Smyrnaeans*, 7.1) since sacraments are symbolic representations of earthly realities.

Mosaic law required that at least two witnesses agree for a fact to stand (see Deut. 17:6, 19:5). The author of 1 John summons three, personalizing them with the masculine plural article (*hoi*, v. 7) although all three are neuter nouns. He calls on water and blood in addition to Spirit to testify to the faith of his community. In the same way, Jesus frequently calls on witnesses in GJohn. The evangelist summons many, the verb "to testify" occurring thirty-three times, the corresponding noun fourteen. So it was done in Jewish courts of law. The testimony of God is greater, 1 John avers, for besides the Spirit that is very God, the water and the blood in which Jesus was sent corroborate the Spirit's reliable witness.

Some zealous copyist of manuscripts in the Old Latin tradition, the version which preceded St. Jerome's Vulgate and was used by St. Augustine and the Western church fathers before Jerome, added this clause (Latin, *comma* = "clause") after the now brief because truncated v. 7:

5 ⁷There are three that testify: [in heaven: Father, Word, and Holy Spirit, and these three are one. ⁸And there are three who give testimony on earth] the Spirit and the water and the blood, and these three are of one accord.

The bracketed parts above represent the clause not found in the authentic Greek text. Obviously, the copyist thought he saw an implicit reference to the divine Trinity here and decided to make it explicit. The clause was adopted in the printed editions of the

Vulgate that had the patronage of Popes Sixtus V (1590) and Clement VII (1592). Erasmus had omitted the *comma Ioanneum,* as it is commonly called, from his editions of the Greek New Testament of 1516 and 1519 but yielded to pressure to reinstate it in 1522. The entire Greek textual tradition knew nothing of it until the twelfth century, when it appeared in the Codex Regius as a marginal gloss. Its inauthenticity was long suspected in the West, despite the fact that it may even date to the late second century in North Africa and plays a part in the history of the Vulgate. The Douai-Rheims Version of 1610 contained it as did the Authorized Version of 1611, even though the title page of the latter says "Translated out of the Original Tongues." It is still there in printed King James Bibles.

Despite the attempt of the original inserters to make the doctrinal point that the three divine persons are co-equal, the clause fails as allegory. The Holy Spirit giving testimony along with the Father and the Word in heaven is set in parallel with a spirit that gives testimony on earth. The incorporator of the gloss into verse 7 must have thought of the "spirit" of the Greek text as a creature along with water and blood. Such would be demanded if all three were to give earthly testimony as a counterpart to the heavenly testimony of the divine triad.

The "testimony" provided in authentic v. 9 is described as that of God. It is given on earth to those who would deny it. Hence, the question arises, to whom is the testimony in heaven given? The insertion seems to miss the point of this witness on earth, namely, that it is given to the Son as Son of God in whom there is life. This is an earthly matter, a human matter. The Johannine *comma* is planted firmly in heaven for a dogmatic, trinitarian purpose. Not surprisingly, it went on to have a history in heresy when the fourth-century Spanish bishop Priscillian, who seems to have denied the Trinity, made it read differently to suit his own purposes.

But the biblical author will not be deflected from his purpose. He knows that God has testified to the Son (v. 9), not the Word to himself, and that those who believe in the Son rightly have this testimony lodged in their hearts (v. 10). Any who would deny this witness make a liar of God, says the author as he re-

turns to the accusatory language of 2:22. He is of the truth party
and that is all there is to it.

The section concludes with a recapitulation of previous affirmations about what the testimony consists in. Eternal life is in
the Son. God has given this life to us. Possessing the Son of God
is identical with having life (vv. 11–12).

The Conclusion, or Epilogue

5 **13**I write these things to you who believe in the name of the
Son of God, so that you may know that you have eternal life.

14And this is the boldness we have in him, that if we ask
anything according to his will, he hears us. **15**And if we know
that he hears us in whatever we ask, we know that we have
obtained the requests made of him. **16**If you see your brother
or sister committing what is not a mortal sin, you will ask, and
God will give life to such a one — to those whose sin is not
mortal. There is sin that is mortal; I do not say that you should
pray about that. **17**All wrongdoing is sin, but there is sin that is
not mortal.

18We know that those who are born of God do not sin, but
the one who was born of God protects them, and the evil one
does not touch them. **19**We know that we are God's children,
and that the whole world lies under the power of the evil one.
20And we know that the Son of God has come and has given
us understanding so that we may know him who is true; and
we are in him who is true, in his Son Jesus Christ. He is the
true God and eternal life.

21Little children, keep yourselves from idols.

This treatise in letter form now comes to a close. The "little
children" to whom it is addressed are assumed to be believers in
the Son of God, but the writer cannot be sure that they know
what their possession of "eternal life" means (v. 13). The phrase
is from John's Gospel; this is a John community. Because of the
many obscurities in that writing by which this author and his
hearers attempt to live, he is quite in order to make an expo-
sition of its central theme. GJohn is at pains to spell out what

correct faith in the one he characteristically calls "the Son" is. It describes him as one who was with the Father as an utterance, a spoken word, of God in the beginning, who came to earth "from above" as human. In his humanity he both was and was not marked by ordinary human limitations. Lengthy discourses are placed on Jesus' lips by the evangelist that indicate his strong desire to return to the Father from whom he has come. While he was with his disciples and addressing the crowds — most often in GJohn, the Jerusalem crowds — he spoke of having come to bring from his Father the gift of life.

At times the Jesus of GJohn terms it "eon life," a phrase derived from Daniel 12:2. That book of prophecy speaks of the everlasting shame or disgrace of the wicked as contrasted with the everlasting (*aiōnios*) life of the just. In this context of judgment at the end of days, each group will have meted out to it its fitting reward or punishment in the final age (*aiōn*). GJohn leaves undisturbed the Jewish end-time thinking that characterizes every book of this Testament, in the sense that for him these judgments always lie in the future. But he does something different besides. He employs the familiar eschatological phrase "eternal life" (in the philosophically influenced translation of the Greek in all the modern vernaculars) to denote a present condition open to believers in Jesus Christ. The entire Gospel has but a single theme. It is belief in him that will result in the gift of that life here and now. The closest GJohn comes to defining or describing it is to speak of it as an abiding (remaining, continuing) in Jesus as Jesus abides in the Father and the Father in him. Whatever the coinherence of these two is and was from the beginning, it is the pattern on which the relation between Jesus' disciples (in GJohn 15:14–15, "friends") and this only Son is modeled. And it begins in this life on condition of belief in him. What that belief is besides acceptance of him as the one who has come from God and abides with believers, this Gospel does not say. That, the author evidently thinks, is enough.

GJohn ends with a lengthy account of Jesus' arraignment before a Roman functionary — a far shorter one before priestly authority — and his sentence to death. He dies on a cross, just as in the other Gospel accounts, and as a result of the same mortal wounds and suffering, but is somehow in complete command of his fate whether in the hands of Pilate or later his executioners. 1 John seems to have been written with a view to interpreting these data in a way clean contrary to another interpretation. A belief in Jesus Christ that leads to eternal life seems common to the two contending parties. The major point of difference is what each makes of an atoning sacrifice in his blood. Was this or was it not what had to be believed in order to achieve the new life that both parties were convinced they had been given?

It is hard to demonstrate definitively that 1 John is doing no more than charging the seceders with a docetic outlook. True, the epistle concedes a "coming from God" to "every spirit that confesses that Jesus Christ has come in the flesh" (4:2). The opponents may believe as much of him. But more than incarnation is at stake. It is not a matter of having human blood that the opposition denies but of the importance to believers of the shedding of this blood to "cleanse us from all sin" (1:7). That is the great point of difference. Did he or did he not come "by blood," meaning not did he come into the world as human but as savior of the world (4:14) by blood, not by water and the Spirit only (5:6)? The other party that this author reviles so roundly may have thought that GJohn chapter 3, Jesus' conversation with Nicodemus, contained the whole salvific message of the gospel. To credit them, it must be acknowledged that the Gospel does not make explicit what is to be believed about the effect of Jesus' tragic end. 1 John interprets it to have been a *hilasmós*, an atoning sacrifice. It argues vigorously against some who have seen no such interpretation as necessary.

Now for a look at the epistle's final recapitulation. It contains most of the elements we might expect but begins, surprisingly, by returning to the assurance expressed in 3:22 that the boldness we have in God and before God's Son means that we will receive anything we ask for (5:14). The earlier passage had made obedience to God's commandments the necessary condition. Here, it is "if we ask anything according to his will." Christian preachers and teachers have been applying this qualification to Jesus' unqualified promise from time immemorial. Only here does it appear in Scripture in so many words. God's simple hearing of our requests — or is it the Son of verses 10–13? (the author might say it made no difference) — is tantamount to receiving a favorable answer (v. 15).

The discussion then takes a darker turn, but there are patches of light. The epistle faces the question of the things that are to be asked for in prayer, more accurately, the persons. There are evidently community members guilty of offenses to whom, in the author's view, God has not yet given the boon of life. Their sins are evidently not "mortal" (NRSV; in other translations "deadly" or "unto death," although all three translations render *pròs thánaton* correctly). For the author there is sin that tends to death and sin that is not deadly. Mind you, he says, all wrongdoing (*adikía,* v. 17; cf. 1:19, where the NRSV calls it "unrighteousness") is sin but here and earlier such sin is described as forgivable. If God can forgive some sin(s), in the view of 1 John, but not other(s), which offenses fall into the two categories? He does not say. Has he provided enough clues to lead us to a satisfactory solution? Well, perhaps, but because interpreters have been arguing over his meaning for centuries up to this very day it cannot be clear.

Verse 16 puts out of bounds praying for forgiveness of a sin that is mortal. In older Bible times the phrase could have meant a sin so corruptive of community life that the sinner had to die. But, so far as we can tell, the death penalty was no longer being leveled for adultery, fornication, or theft as in ancient times; whether for murder we do not know. The death spoken of here is that of the spirit, the opposite of life in the same context. The text does not say that such deadly sin is unforgivable. It simply proposes not praying for such sinners. The implication may be that they are to be left to God at the judgment, in the hope that an interim intervening ostracism may bring them around (see 1 Cor. 5:5: "You are to hand this man over for the destruction of his flesh, so that his spirit may be saved in the day of the Lord"). What can the sin "unto death" be? The prime candidate is the failure to believe and to love that characterizes the secessionists. Certainly the epistle has shown no concern for them up until now except as adversaries. Is this what it means by "mortal sin" — always singular and without an article — the sin the writer has in mind? It may be. But there is no compelling reason to confine it to this one grievous wrong.

In fact, seeing a believer commit "what is not a mortal sin" (v. 16) supposes that the sinner is still a community member and not someone who has departed the ranks. Well, then, is the opposite of mortal sin those everyday failings so open to divine pardon (*venia*) that they came to be called "venial"? The non-mortal wrongdoing (*adikía*) seems to be a more serious matter than everyday shortcomings and failures. Minor offenses do not require intercession on the part of brothers and sisters that God should give them life (v. 16b). Perhaps the distinction is between deliberate sin in a matter so serious that it could lead to the soul's death, and wrongdoing, the gravity or the deliberateness of which the person is not conscious. Or it may be the difference between grave enough lapses and a persistence in sin, the contumely of Hebrews 11:26. We shall have to leave the matter there, for no certainty about the author's meaning is forthcoming. Some penitential discipline familiar to the letter's recipients is being alluded to, but we do not know what was involved.

The next three verses (18–20) begin, "We know," and provide assurance of salvation through freedom from sin for all who are born of God. The rendering of v. 18b in the NRSV, "but the one who was born of God protects them," opts for Jesus as the pro-tector of all others born of God. The construction is confusing but it appears to be a case of Semitic syntax in Greek, in which the second clause depends on the first as in John 17:2. Thus, the better translation seems to be: "rather, God protects the one begotten by him, and so the evil one cannot touch him" (NAB, 1970). Despite the all-pervasive influence of the evil one (v. 19b; cf. 3:8, 10), he cannot touch those who know they are God's chil-dren. The Son of God has come to vanquish him because he is uniquely true (*alēthinós*, v. 20). We are in this Son, Jesus Christ.

A remaining question of considerable importance is whether 1 John closes with the declaration that Jesus Christ is the true God, for if it does it is the only unequivocal statement to that ef-fect in all twenty-seven books. The third "we know" says that the Son of God "has come," using a verb that normally has conno-tations of the parousia and in John 8:42 describes Jesus' coming into the world. The understanding that he came to provide was to help us know that God is "true." This is the adjective favored by GJohn to convey what is real or genuine because divine. Because of this knowledge we are present in God, an expression reminiscent of John 17:21: "Just as you, Father, are in me and I in you, *that they also may be in us.*" In the phrase, "and we are in him who is true, in his Son Jesus Christ" (v. 20c), could the second member be in simple apposition to the first? Such was the theory of the KJV translators, who supplied *even* as a link. But in such case there would be no advance in the thought: Jesus Christ is the one who is true, the "him" of the previous phrase. But that reading does not make sense, since the one just spoken of who is true (20b) is obviously God. Therefore, a meaningful translation requires some linking expression such as, "and we are in him who is true [God] . . . [for (or inasmuch as) we are] in his Son Jesus Christ." It is the latter reality that accounts for the former. We abide in God because we have life in Christ.

The climactic statement of the entire epistle comes at the end: "He [the demonstrative pronoun *houtós;* Jesus Christ has just been mentioned] is the true God and eternal life." This life that was with the Father has been revealed to us, says 1:2. Now it is said that he is that life because he is very God. Predicating deity of Jesus Christ should not come as a total surprise because many passages in GJohn intimate as much. Now it is said without ifs or ands.

The closing warning against idols (v. 21) seems out of place. What can it mean as addressed to a community of believers? It is probably an emphatic parting shot saying "Avoid sin!" Again, the *Testaments of the Twelve Patriarchs* and the Qumrân scrolls, where the word for "idol" in the plural is common in Greek and Hebrew respectively, come to our assistance. The major sin conceivable would, of course, be apostasy, but the author probably has in mind the full range of grievous sins to which the members may fall victim. His final word is: "Avoid them all."

Chapter Two

The Second Letter of John

The First Epistle of John has none of the characteristics of a letter of the ancient world except, perhaps, its repeated direct address "little children" (*teknía*) as contrasted with the more usual "brothers" (*adelphoí*), used in direct address only in 1 John 3:13. The Second and Third Epistles more obviously fit into this literary category. Each is headed by an identification of the sender — "the elder" in both cases — and a recipient, respectively "the elect lady" and Gaius. The two letters end with a near identical penultimate paragraph and with greetings from "children" or "friends" transmitted through the sender to the "lady" receiver (2 John) as to Gaius and "the friends there" (3 John).

If the First Epistle had a wider audience in view than the second two — that is, no single congregation of believers — the others are more narrowly directed. They breathe a certain intimacy and directness found in St. Paul's letter to Philemon but in no other New Testament epistolary writings. Like Philemon, 2 and 3 John each occupy less than a printed page. Whatever the writer's self-designation as "the elder" meant, it would have been known to those who heard the epistle read out. It could have designated an older person (upward of fifty in the ancient world) or someone not so old but venerable on another count, say for his leadership role. He may have been known as *the* elder to a specific congregation.

In any case, the writer speaks with the same authoritative voice as is heard in 1 John. He uses many of the same phrases, a fact that has led to the supposition that all three epistles have come from the same hand. A minority opinion attributes 2 and

3 John to a writer who models himself on the style of 1 John —
perhaps an associate become successor in his circle or school.
But it is more commonly held that the likenesses of vocabulary
and style among all three are the work of the same writer, who
in turn knows GJohn well and the tradition that produced it and
patterns himself on it.

The opinion was common up until early in this century that
the evangelist himself wrote these epistles as part of a follow-up
polemic, but the differences in substance are enough to make
most John scholars deny this. The situation attended to in 1, 2,
and 3 John, however, gives every indication of having arisen in
a community well familiar with John's Gospel and of being a direct response to some erroneous conclusions arrived at by some
who have seceded from the community in the next generation.
As to the identity of the presbyter or elder, it has been thought
in the past that Papias (early second century) provided a clue in
the fragment of his lost, five-book *Sayings of the Lord Explained.*
As Eusebius reports him in his *Church History* (3.39.3–4), Papias
sets out to transmit the interpretations he has carefully learned
from the presbyters (or elders). On encountering anyone who
has known them he questions these hearers to learn "what Andrew or Peter had said, or Philip or Thomas or James or John
or Matthew, or any other disciple of the Lord, and what Aristion
and the presbyter John, disciples of the Lord, are still saying." Papias preferred "a living and abiding voice" to anything written,
which is fine if what abides in that voice is the original message.
All that this gives us, unfortunately, is that there was a second-
or perhaps third-generation elder named John whose report Papias thought he could depend on. But John was a common Jewish
name held by numerous Greek-speaking believers in Jesus, so we
are no farther along.

There simply is no useful external witness to the authorship
of these three epistles. We shall do better to note that attribution
of them as of the Gospel to John, son of Zebedee, is undoubtedly
what assured all four of these writings a place in the canon. Exactly what that link was we do not know. The claim that the
anonymous "disciple whom Jesus loved" is the one whose testimony stands behind all that is contained in GJohn ("the disciple

who is testifying to these things," 21:24) is a complicating rather than a resolving factor in this puzzle. We do well to turn to the text of 2 John to see what it reveals, for speculation about the identity of the elder will not prove productive.

Address and Introductory Phrasing

¹The elder to the elect lady and her children, whom I love in the truth, and not only I but also all who know the truth, ²because of the truth that abides in us and will be with us forever:
³Grace, mercy, and peace will be with us from God the Father and from Jesus Christ, the Father's Son, in truth and love.

The words "love" (noun and verb) and "truth" are characteristic of Johannine thought and occur early in this writing. Whoever authored it, he is confident that the recipients will recognize immediately who "the elder" is. The identity of the "elect lady" (*eklektē̄ kyría*, a dative of reference) is similarly hidden from us. We only know that "elect" or "chosen" is not a woman's given name, viz. the Lady Electa, because the adjective will occur again in v. 13 applied to "sister," there meaning a believer or believers corporately rather than a sibling. In both canonical and extra-canonical writings of the first generations early Christians referred to themselves as chosen. A phrase in 1 Peter may be helpful here. The NRSV translates 5:13 as "Your *sister church* in Babylon, *chosen together* with you," a somewhat cumbersome rendering of the one-word *syneklektḕ*, "the fellow-chosen" who give the final greetings. The assumption that "fellow" is masculine in all circumstances may account for its avoidance.

That a community of believers is intended in 2 John the farewell phrase (v. 13) makes clear. In it the sender is self-identified as plural: "the children of your elect sister." The ones signing off with their "greetings" (a verb of embrace equally serviceable for leave-taking) are likewise the baptized of another community. The form of address, "lady," is not a complete conundrum either, once we know that cities are grammatically feminine in ancient languages. *Kyría* can have a political connotation as well, just as its Latin equivalent *domina* signified the church in some early patristic writings.

The writer loves the community of believers addressed "in truth" and so do all who know this truth that he possesses (v. 1). "In truth" here is not the adverbial "verily" or "sincerely." We know from 1 John 1:18, 2:4, and indeed from GJohn in its entirety what that "truth" is: recognizing Jesus as having come from God in the flesh and, after his return to the Father, continuing to be with us and in us. 1 John adds to GJohn as an essential part of the truth the Son's atoning sacrifice for our sins. This truth "will be with us forever" (1 John 2), something GJohn says several times about the Paraclete and 1 John 2:17 of the life that will be ours without end.

But the introductory matter is not over, for a salutation of "grace, mercy, and peace" is affirmed rather than wished for with regard to the recipients of the letter. 1 and 2 Timothy, both in 1:2, have the same formula, so it must have been widespread. If so it is an expansion of Paul's combination of grace (usual in Greek salutations) and peace in the Hebrew.

> [4]I was overjoyed to find some of your children walking in the truth, just as we have been commanded by the Father. [5]But now, dear lady, I ask you, not as though I were writing you a new commandment, but one we have had from the beginning, let us love one another. [6]And this is love, that we walk according to his commandments; this is the commandment just as you have heard it from the beginning — you must walk in it.

There is no implication in v. 4 that some of the chosen of this other community have *not* been walking in the truth, only that the elder has lately encountered some who have. He is delighted at the discovery. Having received a commandment from the Father, called a "walking in the truth" in the fashion of certain Qumrân phrases (v. 4), the community addressed (*kyría* stands alone; the "dear" is added for euphony in English, as in "*gentle reader*") is urged to mutual love among its members. But this is the commandment they have always had (v. 5; cf. 1 John 2:7, 3:11, 4:7). The two are one, love for one another and keeping the commandments of Jesus that are at the same time of God. The "it" they must walk in is love (v. 6). This is the *hodós,* or way, in which they should proceed (see 1 Kings 2:3; 2 Kings 20:3, where the "walking" verb *peripateîn* of 2 John 6 occurs in the Septuagint). About the awkward construction of the Greek in v. 6c, "this is the commandment...[that] you must walk in it," nothing much can be done except begin a new clause at "you," as is done by the NRSV and other translations.

A WARNING AGAINST THOSE WHO HAVE GONE
BEYOND THE TEACHING

> [7]Many deceivers have gone out into the world, those who do not confess that Jesus Christ has come in the flesh; any such person is the deceiver and the antichrist! [8]Be on your guard, so that you do not lose what we have worked for, but may receive a full reward. [9]Everyone who does not abide in the teaching of Christ, but goes beyond it, does not have God; whoever abides in the teaching has both the Father and the Son.

Those who receive this letter must walk in the commandment, the second phrase of v. 6, *because* (*hóti,* not translated in the NRSV) many deceivers have not. How many are these deceivers (*plánoi,* an adjective used substantively here) who have gone out into "the world," in the pejorative sense of every place that the Johannine believers are not? There is no way to tell—too many, certainly, to suit the writer. Some commentators have taken "many" to indicate that those faithful to the tradition are in the minority and the departers the greater number. The second-century triumphs of gnostic Christianity may suggest such a view but not the word "many" taken by itself. As to their denial regarding Jesus Christ, there can be no doubt why it receives such vigorous censure (v. 7; cf. 1 John 2:18–19, 4:3). Since "antichrists" and the "last hour" are the rhetoric of eschatology, we are prepared for the "Be on guard" of v. 8, a phrase on Jesus' lips in places like Matthew 24:4 and Mark 4:24. There, as an end-time warning, the imperative *blépete* is correctly rendered "Take heed" (AV) or "Beware" (NRSV). The deceit so roundly spoken against has to be a failure to assert the christological faith of the John circle, here primarily concerned to affirm the reality of Jesus Christ as fully human. We are right to call the opponents docetists without knowing precisely what subtle distinctions their teaching embraced. The present participle "coming" of v. 7 usually refers in the Second Testament to Jesus' coming in the future as Lord of glory, but there is no reason it should not have been used to describe the incarnation, as in John 1:14. Later, Ignatius of Antioch in the same tradition will require the confession that he was "clothed in flesh" (*sarkophóron*) as the condition of not "blaspheming my Lord" (*To the Smyrnaeans* 5.2). The elder, speaking for local church A, feels constrained in a letter to local church B to deplore the continuing defection of local church(es) C C¹ C². He warns the participants of the possibility of their losing what they have worked so hard to achieve. The full reward they hope for may elude them (v. 8), namely, of life with the Son and the Father. Again, as has been said of 1 John 3:2–3 above (p. 32), the futurist eschatology of Jewish thought is never absent from the Johannine writings. God quite simply *will* reward the just when the Son who was first sent in the flesh comes in glory.

The phrase "going beyond" the teaching of Christ (*proágōn*) rather than "remaining in" it (*ménōn en*) as received in the tradition has led to the description of the dissidents as "progressives." Most progressives in a movement are a vanguard exploring new frontiers, but when they progress past a core teaching that may not be abandoned, however sublime they may think their new position, they cannot be praised. Is the "teaching of Christ" (v. 9) that which he gave in his lifetime, as in John 7:16 and 18:19, or is it the teaching about him that the Johannine tradition transmits? We may not be able to resolve this. The elder might say that the two are one and not to be separated by the rules of a subjective or objective genitive case. He who taught must not be departed from in his teaching, nor may there be any "progress beyond" the basic truth that this teacher has come from God in the flesh. The unusual phrase, "having" God, both the Father and the Son (v. 9), has already occurred in 1 John 2:23 with respect to the Father and 5:12 as regards the Son. It is a stark way of saying that denial of the community's traditional position on christology will mean loss of the intimate relation with the two that adhering to the tradition ensured. All in all, v. 9 closely resembles 1 John 2:22–23 in saying that apostasy from a once held faith stance means loss of the abiding divine presence.

THE ACTION THAT MUST FOLLOW CONVICTION

[10]Do not receive into the house or welcome anyone who comes to you and does not bring this teaching; [11]for to welcome is to participate in the evil deeds of such a person.

The practical consequence of such theoretical censure is that ostracism is to be enjoined on the offenders (v. 10). The elder is confident he speaks for community A in putting community B on notice that they are not to entertain unwarily any adherents to the reprobated positions espoused by Community C. The measure is meant to protect the faith of the elect lady B against contamination, much as St. Paul hoped to protect God's temple, which was the Corinthian community, against destruction by the influence of any fools within it (1 Cor. 3:17). He instructed those believers to call an assembly in his spirit and solemnly turn the unnamed offender over to Satan for his "salvation in the day of the Lord" (5:3–5). The Qumrân community may have received such treatment at the hands of temple Jewry. Certainly the GJohn people thought themselves ejected from the gatherings of other Jews (see John 9:22, 12:42, 16:2). There is ample evidence in later Christian writings such as the *Didaché*, Irenaeus, and Tertullian that the faithful were regularly warned against association with heretics.

The command to avoid evil companions was there from the beginning of the new groups whose life was Christ, but it early took the form of eschewing those who deviated in doctrine. This was especially true of those devoted to gnostic positions. It was shortly extended to the monarchians and other kinds of modalists, to the followers of Arius and Macedonius, and to any who held heretical positions on ministry or the sacraments. Modern readers need not be reminded of the ostracism by Jews of family members who become Christians, of Catholics who "marry outside the church" or take a second spouse, or the shunning technique practiced by certain anabaptist churches. The motivation in such cases has always been ambivalent as it is in the New Testament: to protect the faithful from people of corrupt morals or who hold false doctrines and to bring offenders to their senses. All such disciplinary measures are medicinal in intent rather than punitive and intended to be temporary until the person has a change of heart. In the case of Orthodox Jews the reason is different. The convert to Christianity is thought to have gone over to the enemy; hence it is apostasy from peoplehood that has cut the convert off from family and friends, not the Jewish people from the apostate.

The stringency of these disciplines is incomprehensible to many of our contemporaries who cannot imagine a religious conviction that one could hold so dear. When they hear of a case of religious avoidance or expulsion, not to say learn of it on the larger stage of Christian history, they are stunned and characterize it as cruel or heartless behavior. It requires being fully committed to something perceived as a great truth of God before an insight into such behavior is possible. Parents are on guard against the violation of their children by sexually corrupt adults, but the reasons for isolating them from certain other adults are down to a few. The protection is almost always in the moral order, seldom against the baleful effects of wrong ideas. Agitation for the banning of public or school library books (usually the wrong ones) constitutes an exception. But in an age when it was assumed that ideas had consequences, such banning or shunning was a commonplace. "For to welcome [anyone who comes to you and does not bring this teaching] is to participate in the evil deeds of such a person" (2 John 10–11). They are not evil deeds of immoral behavior, note, but of deceptive and corrupting thought.

A Personal Visit in Prospect; Farewell

12Although I have much to write to you, I would rather not use paper and ink; instead I hope to come to you, and talk with you face to face, so that our joy may be complete.
13The children of your elect sister send you their greetings.

The elder's intention to visit the "chosen" (v. 1) community at a later date is clearly stated, but more may lie behind it than is said. Face-to-face communication has an advantage over the ink on paper of v. 12. One can spell out emotions and convictions in speech in a way that is not possible in a brief, hortatory letter. The element of exhortation is key here. The letter writer hopes that his joy may be made complete by a personal visit (see v. 12). Is it in fact a confrontation? He has asked the church to which he addresses himself that they love one another, walk in the commandment they have heard from the beginning (vv. 5, 6). Is this conventional speech among Johannine leaders to their congregants, the exhortation of 1 John 1:4 reiterated in so many words, and nothing more? Or does the self-designated presbyter know that he has to visit the elect lady we have called community B to close in a few gaps of mutual love? It is impossible to be sure. Best to say that this is a follow-up letter in the spirit of the first — the writer may have sent many such — which has as its stated purpose preparing the recipients for an imminent visit. The tone is not harsh. Nothing has been penned to render the elect lady apprehensive, no new warnings or threats issued. That other community already well knew where the mother church stood on false christological teaching. The only new element was the instruction not to receive into their houses people who once again are called the antichrist.

Having expressed the hope for a fuller joy, the letter-writer concludes with the transmission of greetings from his own sister church.

Chapter Three

The Third Letter of John

¹The elder to the beloved Gaius, whom I love in truth.

²Beloved, I pray that all may go well with you and that you may be in good heath, just as it is well with your soul. ³I was overjoyed when some of the friends arrived and testified to your faithfulness to the truth, namely, how you walk in the truth. ⁴I have no greater joy than this, to hear that my children are walking in the truth.

This second epistle from one who calls himself the elder is addressed to an individual named Gaius, not to a community. His was a common name in the ancient world. The Acts of the Apostles records St. Paul as having had a Macedonian traveling companion of that name (19:29) and being joined through Macedonia by still another Gaius from Derbe in southern Lycaonia (20:4). Then, in Romans, there is a Gaius who does not sound like either, who was host to Paul and "to the whole church" in Corinth (Rom. 16:23). He is a man of means, therefore, but also one who bears a name as common as John or Sol or Joe in our urban culture. The sole identification to be established for the recipient of 3 John is that he is important enough in his community to hear from the elder, who in turn expects that the contents of the missive will be shared more widely ("the friends there," v. 15). If the greetings can be transmitted to each by name (ibid.), Gaius's community cannot be very large, a couple of hundred at most.

The greeting has been used in the previous letter, "whom I

love in truth" probably meaning the truth about Christ, not just truly or as a matter of fact. Gaius's fidelity and love have been testified to by "friends" even though they may be strangers to him, so there seems to be no need to exhort him to the practice of love. Verse 2 is a standard expression of hope that the recipient of a letter is prospering physically and spiritually. It is evident that he stands in the relation of a spiritual offspring in some fashion to the elder (as one of "my children," v. 4). In any case, the report the elder has received about him is that he is persevering in the right way, which causes the elder to rejoice greatly (v. 3, the same phrase as in 2 John 4). A note on "friends" in the NRSV translation in vv. 3, 5, and 10 is in order. Upon first encountering it, hearers or readers who know this correspondence well will be struck by its unfamiliarity and wonder if it has escaped them all these years that Jesus' affectionate term for Lazarus in GJohn (11:11) and those whom he had told everything he heard from his Father (15:15) was in the text all along. In fact, of course, it is "brothers" in the genitive and accusative cases. In Greek this means believers in Christ of both sexes but the fact gives little comfort to worshipers who are becoming accustomed to the rendering "brothers and sisters," even though it plays hob with the rhythm of English sentences. Sensitive to the problem of gender, the NRSV team has opted for "friends." Doubtless this was because *adelphoùs(-ōn)* is set in opposition to people who are "strangers" to Gaius (v. 5). It is a fair balance and the rendering is ingenious. One only hopes it does not obscure the fact that "brethren" (the familiar archaic form preserved by Bible translations; "sistren" never got beyond being classified as dialectical usage) is a technical term for believers. Certainly "friends" as contrasted with servants or slaves has that meaning in Jesus' farewell discourse. Obviously the believers who arrived testifying to Gaius's fidelity are members of his community or the elder's.

GAIUS THE SUPPORTER OF ITINERANT BELIEVERS

⁵Beloved, you do faithfully whatever you do for the friends, even though they are strangers to you; ⁶they have testified to

your love before the church. You will do well to send them on
in a manner worthy of God; ⁷for they began their journey for
the sake of Christ, accepting no support from non-believers.
⁸Therefore we ought to support such people, so that we may
become co-workers with the truth.

The letter is chatty and like much personal correspondence
somewhat disjointed. It is not a little puzzling when it speaks of
Diotrephes' relation to the elder's community and to Gaius. The
latter's faithfulness to the central truth of the gospel has been
confirmed by report (v. 3). This doctrinal firmness is matched
by a fidelity in the exercise of service. When believers who hold
the convictions of the elder and Gaius pass through the latter's
place of residence, he receives them hospitably before sending
them on their way. These are obviously itinerant evangelists proclaiming the authentic gospel. They will accept no support from
Gentiles (*ethnikõn*, v. 7) who are not Christians if they are offered it. The people who deserve the support of the writer and
receiver of the epistle are clearly another group, but they enjoy
the approval of both. One thinks of the approbation and support modern evangelizers are accorded by people and clergy who
are stably located and who are fully aware of the faith creden-
tials of the missionaries. From earliest times men and women
who have begun a literal journey "for the sake of the name
[rendered 'Christ' by the NRSV]" have been sent forward on it
in a manner "worthy of God" (vv. 6–7). This passage is rightly
identified with parts of Matthew 10 as forming a charter of
mission activity. The *Didachē* of the late first or early second
century will take up the theme in its chapters 11–13. There, tests
are proposed for distinguishing the genuine apostle, teacher, or
prophet from the false claimants to those roles. Specific direc-
tions are given for sending itinerants on the road after three
days at most and for putting prophets to work who wish to settle in a community. The faith test, just as in 3 John, is whether
the new arrival "proves himself a renegade by teaching otherwise than all that we have been saying [lit., shares perverted
doctrine]" (*Did. 11.2*).

THE INSUBORDINATE AND WORSE DIOTREPHES

9I have written something to the church; but Diotrephes, who likes to put himself first, does not acknowledge our authority. **10**So if I come, I will call attention to what he is doing in bringing false charges against us. And not content with those charges, he refuses to welcome the friends, and even prevents those who want to do so and expels them from the church.

The elder refers in v. 9 to a previously written letter that we do not have. Unless the new paragraph is a complete *non sequitur,* the subject was the treatment of traveling *adelphoí* by "the church," namely, the community of the trusted Gaius and the uncooperative Diotrephes, which is either the same community or in the same area. Diotrephes is described by the participial form of a verb we find only here in Greek literature, though a cognate noun and adjective occur. He is a "putting-himself-first" individual and the elder resents it, not only as a character trait but because its practical effect is that "he does not accept our [viz., the elder's] authority" (v. 9). This means that he acts independently, whereas the elder thinks he should be subject to him in the matter of receiving the traveling believers (the "friends" of v. 10). The elder does not say why Diotrephes has such a policy. He does not say that his opponent has a different theoretical view of their admissibility, although the drastic act of expulsion may suggest as much. Diotrephes may be a close man with his community's funds and think that its exchequer cannot stand the constant drain imposed by wandering prophets (if that is who the "friends" are), especially when Gaius stands ready to put them up. In a word, there is no warrant for attributing the strain between the elder and Diotrephes to a difference between them on the doctrine of the "brothers/friends."

It could be that the letter writer liked to put *himself* first and was engaging in projection. It is more likely that he thought he possessed spiritual authority over Diotrephes, who thought otherwise. "Jurisdiction" is not a correct term in this early stage of church development, but something like it, an understanding over lines of authority, is surely in question. The Christian tradition has been that the elder had the right of the argument both because of his title, which seems to have been acknowledged, and because his brief missive ended as canonical Scripture. If the epistle is correct in saying that Diotrephes has spread false charges against the elder, then the Christian centuries have been right in viewing him censoriously (see v. 10). But Diotrephes may have thought that the elder was out of order in telling him what to do, or that he had better reasons for turning the brethren away than the elder had for enjoining that they be received. In that case the "false charges" complained of may simply have been Diotrephes' side of the story. It should be noted that we are told the elder's convictions in the matter but not his own practice. We assume that he welcomed the brethren, but he may not have had to put them up for days. We know what Gaius did, for which he is commended. We also know that Diotrephes did not do that, which resulted in his being portrayed as heartless and possibly wrong in faith. If the elder is in an administrative position regarding other churches, sending "co-workers with the truth" (v. 8) out on mission while not having to billet any of them himself, our sympathy for his position may be diminished. Most interpretations of the passage have understood Diotrephes to be self-important as charged, hence insubordinate, and possibly expelling people from the church who hold the Johannine christology that he does not espouse. It may be so, but the evidence is weak.

Adolf von Harnack in his monograph *On the Third Letter of John* (1897) set the itinerant missionaries who looked to the elder for direction in opposition to Diotrephes. He thought him to be the first sole bishop of a community. Some like Wendt and Bauer, writing in the 1920s, viewed Diotrephes as a heretic despite the all but non-existent evidence concerning his doctrinal positions (the "what is evil?" of v. 11). Then the now senior scholar Ernst Käsemann reversed that view by identifying Diotrephes as a spokesman for emerging christological orthodoxy while the party of the elder represented the position of GJohn in its further drift toward gnosticism. He backed up that position, which he took in a 1951 essay, by publishing *The Testament of Jesus: A Study of the Gospel of John in the Light of Chapter 17* (English translation, 1968). That slim book,

first presented as the Shaffer Lectures at Yale, holds that the
Fourth Gospel was committed to a "naïve docetism" and that the
church in missing its point included it in its canon of Scripture
by a happy accident and attributed to it an orthodox reading of
christology that was not there.

The reconstruction Raymond Brown placed on the three
letters done by the same author is found in his massive commentary (1983) but appeared in condensed form in his previously
published *The Community of the Beloved Disciple* (1979). Brown
engaged in a reconstruction of events for which he claimed at
most probability, saying that "if sixty percent of my detective
work is accepted, I shall be happy indeed" (p. 7). If the session-
ists of 1 John can be called children of the devil and antichrists
because of their denial that Jesus has come in the flesh, their
position must be that Jesus was so divine that he was not fully
human, that he does not belong to the world and never did. This
reconstruction is based in good part on what we know of second-
century gnosticism, as foreshadowed by texts like, "Do not love
the world or the things in the world" (1 John 2:15) and "They
are from the world; therefore what they say is from the world
and the world listens to them" (4:5). Brown takes the second-
century development that followed the writing of the epistles to
mean that the world had listened to the secessionists in greater
numbers than heeded the John community. Thus: the numerical
prospering of docetist and other gnostic sects and of Montanist
spiritism with its reliance on the Paraclete as the church's sole
teacher. The latter, Brown thinks, is what some made of 1 John's
insistence that anointing with the Spirit obviates the need for
human teachers. Finally the John party, seeing itself unable to
cope with the secessionists' growth through relying on arguments from tradition, aligned itself with the "great church" that
was developing elsewhere, which looked to presbyter-bishops as
guardians of the tradition and interpreters of the Spirit's action.
The argument has as the two poles of its axis the proliferation
of gnostic sects reported on by Irenaeus in his *Refutation and
Overthrow of the Knowledge Falsely So-Called* (*Adversus Haereses,*
ca. 190) and the few indications in the three epistles that some,
or even many, were departing from the larger Johannine com-

munity because they attributed spirit to Jesus Christ but denied
him flesh.

DEMETRIUS COMMENDED AND THE PROMISE OF A VISIT REPEATED. FINAL GREETINGS

11Beloved, do not imitate what is evil but imitate what is good.
Whoever does good is from God; whoever does evil has not
seen God. 12Everybody has testified favorably about Demetrius, and so has the truth itself. We also testify for him, and
you know that our witness is true.

13I have much to write to you, but I would rather not write
with pen and ink; 14instead I hope to see you soon, and we
will talk together face to face.

15Peace to you. The friends send you their greetings. Greet
the friends there, each by name.

In proceeding to say a kind word about Demetrius, whom
the elder identified only by his favorable reputation, his still
angry thoughts about Diotrephes supply him with an introduction. The axiomatic counsel to avoid evil and do good would be
fairly meaningless if Gaius, here addressed as "beloved," had not
just been provided with a graphic example of bad behavior. To
be "from God" (cf. 1 John 3:10) and to have "seen God" (3:6),
the phrases of 3 John 11, are fairly synonymous. They are found
in GJohn at 8:47 and 14:9 as well as in the longer First Epistle.
To be from God is to do what is right and good. This describes
Demetrius's behavior. "Truth itself" (Christ? the Spirit? perhaps
best of all, the general testimony of the church) confirms what
everyone says of him. And the elder joins the chorus, adding a
phrase like today's "Would I lie to you?": "And you know that
our testimony is true" (v. 12b).

The decision not to write any further but to visit at an early
opportunity is expressed in 3 John 13–14 in words almost identical to those in 2 John 12. For those convinced they were written
in the sequence of their enumeration, the author of 3 John has
repeated almost verbatim what he said in 2 John. But not all
are satisfied that they were written in that order. Charles Tal-

bert goes so far as to hold in *Reading John* (1992) that the three epistles were written before the Gospel in its final form and that 2 John is the only genuine letter. He goes on to hypothesize that 3 John was written from it in simulated letter form and 1 John, written later still, makes no bones about being a treatise rather than a piece of correspondence.

In any case, the "friends" of 3 John 15 who send Gaius greetings are the same as the "children of your elect sister" of 2 John 13, namely, the community members in whose name the elder dashes off his brief letters. Both are protective and warning in tone and one is hostile to a specific individual.

Bibliography

Black, Clifton. "1, 2, and 3 John." *The New Interpreters' Bible.* Vol. XII. Nashville: Abingdon, forthcoming.

Brown, Raymond E. *The Gospel According to John,* i–xii and xiii–xxi. Anchor Bible 29 and 29a. Garden City, N.Y.: Doubleday, 1966, 1970.

————. *The Community of the Beloved Disciple.* New York/Mahwah, N.J.: Paulist, 1979.

————. *The Epistles of John.* Anchor Bible 30. New York: Doubleday, 1982.

Bruce, F. F. *The Epistles of John.* Grand Rapids, Mich.: William B. Eerdmans, 1970.

Bultmann, Rudolf. *The Gospel of John: A Commentary.* Philadelphia: Westminster, 1971.

————. *The Johannine Epistles.* Hermeneia. Philadelphia: Fortress, 1973. 2d German ed., 1967.

Dodd, C. H. *The Johannine Epistles.* London: Hodder and Stoughton, 1946.

Grayston, Kenneth. *The Johannine Epistles.* New Century Bible. Grand Rapids: Eerdmans, 1984.

Houlden, J. L. *A Commentary on the Johannine Epistles.* Harper's New Testament Commentaries. New York: Harper and Row, 1973.

Lieu, Judith. *The Theology of the Johannine Epistles.* New Testament Theology, gen. ed. J. D. G. Dunn. Cambridge: Cambridge University Press, 1991.

O'Day, Gail R. "John." *The New Interpreter's Bible.* Vol. IX. Nashville: Abingdon, 1995.

Perkins, Pheme. "The Johannine Epistles," 61. *New Jerome Biblical Commentary.* R. E. Brown, J. A. Fitzmyer, R. E. Murphy, eds. Englewood Cliffs, N.J.: Prentice Hall, 1989.

————. "The Gospel According to John," 62. *New Jerome Biblical Commentary.* R. E. Brown, J. A. Fitzmyer, R. E. Murphy, eds. Englewood Cliffs, N.J.: Prentice Hall, 1989.

Schnackenburg, Rudolf. *The Gospel According to St. John.* Vol. 1, chapters 1–4. New York: Herder and Herder, 1968. Vol. 2, chapters 5–12, and Vol. 3, chapters 13–21. New York: Crossroad, 1982.

———. *The Johannine Epistles: Introduction and Commentary.* New York: Crossroad, 1992. 7th German ed., 1984.

Smalley, Stephen S. *1, 2, 3 John.* Word Biblical Commentary. Waco: Word Books, 1984.

Smith, D. Moody, *First, Second, and Third John.* Interpretation. Louisville: John Knox, 1991.

Talbert, Charles H. *Reading John: A Literary and Theological Commentary on the Fourth Gospel and the Johannine Epistles.* New York: Crossroad, 1992.

Index of Biblical Passages

Index of Extra-Biblical References

Index of Names

Gerard S. Sloyan is a priest of the diocese of Trenton, N.J., and Professor Emeritus of Religion at Temple University. He is currently a professorial lecturer in the School of Religious Studies at the Catholic University of America. His most recent book is *The Crucifixion of Jesus: History, Myth, Faith* (1995).